Somers...

From Mouths of Men

From Mouths of Men

George Ewart Evans

There I heard,
From mouths of men obscure and lowly, truths
Replete with honour;
Wordsworth, *The Prelude*. XIII, 182–4

FABER AND FABER LIMITED
3 Queen Square London

First published in 1976
by Faber and Faber Limited
3 Queen Square London WC1
Printed in Great Britain by
Ebenezer Baylis and Son Ltd
The Trinity Press
Worcester, and London

ISBN 0 571 10771 0

εἰς ἐμοί ἄνθρωπος τρισμύριοι· οἱ δ' ἀνάριθμοι οὐδείς.

(One man to me is a crowd: the uncounted mass is beyond my ken)
The Palatine Anthology

From a different line of work, my colleagues,
I bring you an idea. You smirk.
It's in the line of duty. Wipe off that smile, and
as our grandfathers used to say:
Ask the fellows who cut the hay.

The Decade of Sheng Min : Ezra Pound's version

Yn cofio
Dafydd Aubrey Thomas

Contents

———————— ✳ ————————

Contents

Illustrations

————————— ✳ —————————

Acknowledgements

---------------------------------- ✳ ----------------------------------

I am greatly indebted to all those men and women who have given me information for the making of this book, and also for the enjoyable hours I have spent in conversation with them. My thanks are also due to a number of friends whose names are not mentioned in the text: especially Mr Morley Kennerley who read the book in manuscript and made some valuable suggestions; Mr and Mrs Stewart Meek, Mr M. H. V. Fleming, Mrs Elaine Strutt, Mr Roger Frith, Mr Eric Fowler, the late Mrs Phillis Cunnington, Miss Anne Buck lately Curator of Platt's Hall Museum, Mrs M. Frey and Mr Douglas Matthews of the London Library. I owe a particular debt of gratitude to Mr Douglas Miller who gave me great help in getting material for the mining chapters and made some necessary corrections in the manuscript. My thanks are also due to Mr James G. Delaney for his help and advice.

I wish to thank Lord Rhodes for permission to use material for which he holds the copyright, and all those authors and their publishers who allowed me to quote from their writings: the late The Rt. Hon. R. H. S. Crossman and *The Listener*; Professor Hugh Trevor-Roper, *The Listener* and Athlone Press; Professor W. G. Hoskins and the Centaur Press; Mr A. J. P. Taylor, *The Listener* and *The Times Literary Supplement*; Mr Theodore Roszak and Faber and Faber; and Sir Anthony Richard Wagner and Oxford University Press.

My thanks are due to those who gave me use of photographs: Norwich Libraries for Plate 1; Mr W. R. Ward for Plates 2 and 3; Mrs M. Parker for Plates 4, 5 and 6; Mr L. C. K. Reynolds for Plates 9 and 15; Mr Bob Spindler for Plate 7; Mr A. J. George for Plate 8; to Birmingham Public Libraries, Local Studies Department for their courtesy in allowing me to reproduce Plate 16; The National Museum of Wales for Plates 17 and 18; Mr T. J. Davies for Plate 19 and Mr Chris Evans for Plate 20. I should also like to thank Mr George Evans of Banwen for his drawing of the

Acknowledgements

drift-mine and for the sketches of mining operations on which the illustrations by Mr Peter Branfield are based.

Finally, I record my thanks to my publishers—especially to Mr Michael Wright, Mrs Elizabeth Renwick and Mrs Shirley Tucker—who once again have given their usual care and attention to the production of another of my books.

Part One
The Town

I

The Depth of Oral History

———————— ✳ ————————

This book is about the use and study of oral evidence taken from people who have lived sufficiently long to be able to talk about a period of their lives that already has an unassailable claim to be treated as historical. Many of the reasons why oral testimony is valuable in the study of history have been discussed in a previous book[1] where there were also numerous examples—chiefly from the countryside—of the kind of oral source that has been available. I do not propose to repeat the discussion here, although in the pages that follow it may well be touched upon again. What I hope to do in the present book is to illustrate how the method suggested and illustrated in the previous book, which was concerned mainly with the countryside, can be used to collect examples of oral sources in the town, the city and in industry.

Before going on to do this, however, I feel I should record the conviction that gradually grew upon me while working on these two books, as it may induce the reader to look from a fresh angle at the material set down. It seems to me now that the value of oral history, as it has come to be called, is not so much in the new material it can reveal, although this is manifestly of great importance, as in the bringing home to the student or researcher a new consciousness of history which is entirely different from the knowledge or enlightenment he can obtain through the conventional methods. It has been well said that unless a student of history has a lively knowledge of and relationship with the present it is not possible for him to see the past in a fruitful way. Whether he is conscious of it or not, the present is his δός ποῦ στῶ, the point of leverage that enables him to prise out the solutions to the problems he has set himself in his attempts to understand the past. And in assessing anything that has happened in a distant time, or in estimating any character who figures in its annals, his main and

[1] *The Days That We Have Seen,* Faber and Faber, 1975.

safest point of reference will be his knowledge of an analogous happening in his own time, or of a person he himself knows or one who has repeatedly revealed himself in print or through the media. For it may be axiomatic that the historian has to learn how different the past is from the present, but it is also equally clear that to establish particular differences he has to have a fair appreciation of the shape of things in his chosen field as they exist and act upon one another today. The present therefore is one of the keys to the past, and familiarity with it is one of the historian's valuable assets. It is valuable not simply for the pragmatic reason that he can find perhaps fortuitous or mechanical correspondences between what has happened before and what is in the news today. It is important because he can learn from the present the questions to ask of the past and of the evidence he has about it; and, not least, for the reason that he can then begin to fix the past—as yet only provisionally—in his own imagination. This in many ways will be his most difficult task, for getting at the facts—his technique—is a straightforward exercise compared with arriving at an understanding of their inter-relation: how they were constellated, how (to change the figure) at their synapse nodes they communicated with and reacted upon one another during the period he has set himself to study.

In addition to a general apprehension of the present which is there for the student to acquire, he has also at this time access to people who are themselves living bridges to the past. The oldest generation of people now alive matured in an entirely different era from the present; and he can learn from them not only the facts about their way of life at that time but the feel of the whole environment they grew up in. As this was a historical environment, having remained, up to the recent Break,[1] essentially the same for centuries this experience can become of inestimable value to him both as a historian and a man. A small but telling example suggests itself from the book already mentioned, where oral evidence from a former herring fisherman included this sentence: 'These men had to be skilled enough to *beat the nets*.'[2] This dialect phrase, taken out of the context of herring fishing off the East Anglian coast of a half-century ago, immediately links this period with the fourteenth century. For Chaucer used exactly

[1] ibid., pp. 15–19.
[2] ibid., p. 182, repair the nets.

the same phrase in listing the abilities of a character—the Miller of Trumpington—in the *Canterbury Tales*:[1]

> *Pypen he coude and fisshe, and nettes bete*

We get therefore from this simple dialect phrase a glimpse of the historical depth that existed in the occupations we have taken so much for granted, and it provides us with another example of the essential continuity in the history or the folk-life of a region extending well over six hundred years right up to the recent past. It also points rather dramatically to the relevance that the near-present, the historical foreground, has to the distant past: that is, to an area that a student either of history or language can fruitfully explore. A student of Middle English, for instance, can acquire through the dialect and its social context, which is available from the older generations, a vivid appreciation of the bare meaning of these fourteenth-century words, and more importantly, an inkling of the whole temper of life, the precise social field in which the people lived this life and how they themselves viewed it. Following this expansion of his terms of reference to include the dialect's historical context at the beginning of this century he is enabled to go far beyond the mere rendering of a Middle English word into its modern counterpart. By gaining something more than its lexical equivalent, and by placing the word in its niche in a rich human context that it has now been possible for him partially to re-create, he can arrive at an approximation to a true translation, a full understanding of the word and the harmonics that its original usage generated. This is what I take to be the meaning of George Steiner's phrase *internal translation*, implying a full understanding of a language at a past stage in its development.[2]

A couplet by the poet John Clare gives us another example of how important it is, in order fully to understand a text, to have a knowledge of the whole way of life—the material culture as well as the oral tradition—of the time when the text was written. The quotation is from *The Shepherd's Calendar*[3] [July]:

> *From the black smiths shop the swain*
> *Jogs wi ploughshares laid again*

[1] *The Reves Tale*, line 7 (*pypen* .. play on the bag-pipe).
[2] *After Babel*, Chapter One.
[3] Edited by Eric Robinson and Geoffrey Summerfield, Oxford University Press, 1964, p. 91.

The phrase *laid again*, in spite of the careful glossing of the text by the book's editors, has escaped their notice. *Laid*, to Clare and his contemporaries, had in this context a meaning that has since become obsolete: it meant that the worn ploughshares were taken to the smith's to be *laid* or re-edged, a new piece of metal being welded on to the worn section, in readiness for another season of ploughing: here probably, as it was in the month of July, for a ploughing of the fallows—the *long summerlands*. Thus the image of the shining, newly furbished ploughshares, which contributes to the authentic colour of this passage, is lost. Few ploughshares are laid, it seems, today: once they have become worn and blunt they are disposed of in the modern manner.

But to return to the theme of the present book: the taking of oral evidence to supplement and enlighten the history of town or city and the industries linked with them. For my own part it was the accident of coming to live in the Suffolk countryside that at first concentrated my attention exclusively on the history that could be gathered from the people who live in a rural setting. Although I made occasional incursions into the town I was too preoccupied with following my researches in the countryside to give much attention to the taking of oral evidence elsewhere. But, as I later found out, although sources with the greatest historical depth and the most profound implications for the discipline of history are to be found in the rural areas, the town and the city are nevertheless equally rich in a different way, because they too have changed so greatly within the lifetime of most of their inhabitants in such vital activities as transport, building, the crafts, manufacturing, business methods and the various leisure-time activities that have sprung up or been developed during the past few decades.

It may, however, be suggested that the town and the city are, on the surface at least, less promising fields for the oral historian: many towns and most cities have already lost their character through the speed of change and are becoming increasingly de-humanized—so the argument goes. Yet both town and city are much less abstract and impersonal, even after so many changes, than might appear at first acquaintance. Apart from the fact that a town or city is often made up of a jigsaw of little 'villages', the various occupational groups—including the unions, the professional groups such as lawyers, doctors, architects and teachers; the leisure activities groupings, including sport, the theatre, the music hall, the orchestras, the museums—are all human foci and potential sources for the historian. This has been recognized for many years in some centres in Britain, notably: The Institute of Folk Life Studies at the University of Leeds, The School of Scottish Studies at Edinburgh, The Welsh Folk Museum at St Fagan's, Cardiff and The English Department at the University of Sheffield (through John D. A. Widdowson). Some of these centres already have large archives of recorded material which in part relate to urban areas. During the past few years also, the University of Essex oral history project has accumulated, under the direction of Paul and Thea Thompson, a fair-sized collection of urban material on tape. Raphael Samuel at Ruskin College, Oxford, has been fostering through his students oral history projects in town as well as country and so has Anna Davin in East London. At University College, Swansea, the South Wales Coalfield project, along with the recently founded South Wales Miners' Library, is opening up a new and exciting area of research. It also provides a classic demonstration of the importance of oral evidence which is buttressed by only a minimum amount of documentary material, the vast bulk of colliery records having been systematically destroyed at the pit-head by order of the coal owners when the mines were nationalized in 1947.

One fact comes out clearly from the work already done in urban and industrial areas: oral evidence collected there often shows a surprisingly greater historical depth than might have been thought possible in such an environment. Here is an example from an industrial area of Yorkshire: it is tied closely to the woollen industry, and it concerns a family of *clothiers*, hand-loom weavers, who have lived in the Yorkshire valleys, near Saddleworth on the Lancashire border, for at least 350 years. The extraordinary length of the Rhodes family tradition came to light in 1964 when Mr Hervey Rhodes, who had been Labour Member of Parliament for Ashton-under-Lyne for many years, was created a life peer. Sir Anthony Richard Wagner, Garter King of Arms, discovered that Hervey Rhodes had been taught as a boy to recite his family descent. 'I confess,' Sir Anthony writes, 'that this late survival in Industrial England of a seven generation genealogical oral tradition astonished me.'[1] Lord Rhodes, as he says himself, is now as

[1] *English Genealogy* (Second Edition), Oxford University Press, 1972, p. 19.

he has always been: he continues to live near the spot where he was born, and he still has the accent of his native district and he still uses the dialect. In no way has he kicked the ladder away. He tells here part of the story of his family and his own life in the woollen industry.

'I was born in Saddleworth in 1895. My family had been in that area since the seventeenth century—and probably before that. They are traceable in the records at the church. Yes, we had a long oral tradition in our family. Well, short of having a family tree, one of the first things that I was taught, as to who we were and where we came from, was by my father who had himself heard it orally. And he used to tell me that I was Hervey of Jack's of Bill's of Joe's of John's of Thomas's—of Dean Head. That's it! Hervey, that's me, Jack was my father, and his father was Bill's of Joe's of John's of Thomas's. I think that is as it is accurately. It is a bit different from Sir Anthony Richard Wagner's—the one I gave him. The rest of my family knew the pedigree too.

'And, actually, this domestic manufacturing (we called them clothiers in the records) was on both sides of our family. On my mother's side there was a tradition in the family going back to—well, a long long time. My grandfather on my mother's side took me on a walk I remember—I couldn't have been more than five years old—up into the Castleshaw valley; and there he showed me the remains of what he called Johnny's Mill; and he poked among the ruins and then he told me the story. He said that his father was rather a wild man, and had left the district because his father disapproved of him. And in the cotton "panic" in the middle of last century, my grandfather was sent with a hoop and stick over from Huddersfield [about twelve miles] where his father had emigrated to; he was sent over into Delph because the family was starving. And old Johnny who had this little mill sent my grandfather off with a muck-fork and he had to spread the muck on the meadow. Then he sent him off with some black bread and some ham; and he bowled his way all the way back to Yorkshire. That's one of my earliest memories. That was on my mother's side. Of course there was a lot of poverty; a lot of people went into the workhouse in those days. Oh yes, it was a commonly accepted thing that sons wheeled their fathers and mothers in a wheelbarrow to Running Hill workhouse. The Industrial Revolution had a very black side to it. We still got remains of it; but now it has given place to something different.

'Yes, on both sides of my family they were weavers, and they were—shall I say—good ones at it. One of my ancestors went with his stuff to America: they used to put it up in bales, and they would then sleep under the tarpaulin on deck in the wind-jammers going to America. That has come down in the family: in fact there are documents to show that. And they were caught up with the legislation in America to do with Paul Jones, the privateer. William Cobbett, who was a kind of barrack-room lawyer, represented the Saddleworth manufacturers in America, claiming the money because the Americans had impounded this on account of the privateers who were molesting the American ships coming with supplies from France. No, Cobbett wasn't in the army when he was out there at this time. William Cobbett was a sergeant-major, and then he rather languished and left the army.[1] But he was a great man for advocacy, and he represented the Saddle-worth manufacturers, and our lot was part of them. But they manufactured in the attics. The house is still in existence: they had hard labour in that house. The pictures of the last hand-loom weaving factory in existence is in one of Ammon Wrigley's books. I think it is *The Wind Among the Heather* where he describes how the hand-loom weaving industry died in the arms—as he put it— of the Rhodes family. The cloth was milled until it stood upright: it was so thick and stiff. But this was used for coachmen's over-coats. It had to withstand the weather. The stage-coach drivers used to wear that cloth—called broadcloth. It was as stiff as a board.

'The eldest of the family kept the family tradition of hand-loom weaving because it went from father to eldest son; and it came down to 1916 in one of the branches of the Rhodes family. But we weren't of that family. The three brothers who set up in 1603 on the hillside—there were two younger brothers and the eldest one; and my father, our lot, were descendants of one of the younger brothers. When it became obvious that the Industrial Revolution was overtaking hand-loom weaving, they naturally gravitated to the mill; and that is the reason why my father was a mill-worker and why I had to go into the mill when I was twelve: I was a

[1] *The Autobiography of William Cobbett* (Edited by William Reitzel), Faber and Faber, 1967.

woollen worker when I was twelve. I used to *piece-up*—piece threads in the *mule gate*. That was my first job when I was twelve years old—half-time: mornings one week, afternoons the next. And we worked Saturday mornings, if we were on mornings, and we worked five half-days if we were on afternoons. Of course, I used to take papers: I used to run with papers as well. Our wages were 3s 6d a week; and I remember I hadn't been there very long before I worked half an hour overtime. And the man who paid us our wages, the man who was in charge of the mill (he had two *piecers* and I was one, the junior), for half an hour overtime he gave me a ha'penny. At least he said it would be a ha'penny, but he hadn't got change and he gave me a penny. He said:

"Bring me back a ha'penny in the morning."

'This was a Friday, and I told my mother and my mother said:

"All right, I'll give you the ha'penny change in the morning."

'When the morning came, about half past five in the morning and I was ready for setting off to the mill, I said to my mother:

"Oh, what about the ha'penny change for Mr Taylor?"

"Right," my mother said, "now when you get to work offer him these"; and she had in her hand two ha'pennies, "and tell him to pick the biggest."

'Well, I didn't really expect what I got, because when I— when Mr Taylor said:

"Have you brought that ha'penny back, lad?" and I said, "Yes, and my mother said you have to pick the biggest," I got the best clout over the ear I've ever had!

'A piecer's work? If the thread broke on the mule, you had to piece it up, join the ends. You did that by taking out the twist of one and putting the other into it and twisting it in the way which the mill was operating. It's a bit too difficult to explain.

'I came out of the mill and went to Canada in 1912 when I was seventeen, to make my fortune! But unfortunately it coincided with the worst slump they'd ever had: there was a tremendous credit-squeeze on and a lot of people were out of employment. So that didn't come off; and of course I came home. I went back into the—oh no! I went into a foundry then like I'd been in in Canada. And then, a year after I came back from Canada, I joined up— during the second week of the war [August 1914]. I went into the Royal Lancaster Regiment. Later on I was commissioned. And I don't suppose I would have found myself if it hadn't been for the army. They recommended me for a commission where I was in the King's Own Royal Lancaster, and I went to a training school, an OCTU, at St John's College, Cambridge. And it was there that I found my feet, because I came out of—oh, I think it was about 450—I came out fifth in the examination. So I knew then that I had what it took, if only I took the trouble.'

After passing out of OCTU Hervey Rhodes was seconded to the Royal Flying Corps, and he trained as an observer. He later flew in RE8s on the Western Front and was awarded the D.F.C. and Bar. Towards the end of the war he was badly wounded, and he was in hospital for two and a half years after the war finished. He was discharged in 1921 with a partially paralysed right leg and an unhealed wound in the left which remained open for forty years. It had to be dressed twice every day—morning and night. The wound eventually healed up after an operation in 1958: the doctors used a technique that had been discovered and developed during the Spanish Civil War: this involved encasing the wound in plaster of paris and allowing it more or less to heal itself.

'I started my woollen business with £250, war gratuity. I really became a capitalist because I couldn't get work! I was out of work: I was on two sticks and couldn't get a job. My father and brother helped me to build a wooden hut; and I paid one or two £s for some old looms which had been thrown out on the scrap heap. I did them up and ran them myself. That was in 1921 when I began my business. In 1927 I moved to a small mill where there was water because I wanted to do my own *finishing*.[1] And it coincided really extraordinarily because, not knowing a lot about my pro-genitors, in a way—apart from what my father had told me—I was just under the old houses where my family had been brought up. The mill was in a hollow below. That winter, the old people asked me if I would preside at their old people's party which was on the first Saturday in the New Year. So I said, "Yes, I will." There they were! They'd got all sorts of beards and their tail-coats were going green on the shoulders with old age—great rugged characters, marvellous people! And there was I, a comparatively young man, trying to interest them. I started off by saying:

"I suppose you think I'm a foreigner," I said, "I suppose you think that I'm a *comer-in*. But I'll let you know that I'm Hervey of Jack's of Bill's of Joe's of John's of Thomas's—of Dean Head!"

[1] The final stages in making the cloth, especially the fulling.

'Everybody laughed. But one old man got up: his name was Rhodes, too. He was eighty-four then:

"Ah," he says, "the pedigree is *reet* [right] but the place is wrong. Thy lot came from younger end of family, and they lived at what they call Dean Head *Clough*."

'So instead of the trepidation that I'd had, expecting him to contest this pedigree, I really had confirmation of it. But he was putting me in my place as belonging to the younger lot in the family.

'Of course everything went swimmingly after that. The whole district rallied to me when work was very hard to come by; and they were a marvellous lot. I still go back there. I live only a mile away now. I've never been any different. There's a great satisfaction in living and working in the district my family came from—especially standing for Labour. Because my own work people asked me to stand for Labour in 1945. I stood for Labour for the next constituency. And anybody who wants to find their level—how people regard them, or how their standing is in competition with somebody else—a Parliamentary Election is a very educating experience, I can tell you. You can't stand for Labour, for a constituency next door—within a mile—as I did, if there is something wrong with your labour relations. Don't forget!

'And it was remarkable because when I became a peer in 1964 I said to my wife: "We'll go away for a fortnight and see what the reaction is." We came back after the fortnight was over, and I went down into the village to the tobacconist's. I saw across the road a chap who used to work for me. Well, I thought, it shan't be long now before I know how they've taken it! So I went into the tobacconist's and came out, and there he was. And he elbowed me, you know [a nudge with the elbow] to attract my attention. I said, "Hullo!" He said:

"We're *fain* [glad], tha knows. But remember," he said, "it's an honour for district. The district deserves it."

'Well, at that juncture I thought: Is that all there is coming out of it? Because if it was I should be bitterly disappointed.

"But," he said, "we would rather it were thee than anybody." And of course, that was it. It was right: I knew!

'There is another tradition in my family. In all probability I'll be speaking on it next Monday [House of Lords, 10.3.75][1] on the

[1] See Hansard: 11.3.75.

Trade Union Bill. There's a book in our family that's now in the custody of the local historical society. It is really the account book and copy-letter book of a very famous member of the family—old George Rhodes. He lived—oh, about 600 yards from where I live now, on a little farm. But he was an extraordinary character. He had a great capacity: he could hand out invective like nobody's business. He was a hand-loom weaver, and he formed the first hand-loom weavers' union. And the book has all the stuff in it: they paid threepence a week [membership fee] although wages were less than ten shillings. This was in the early part of last century. (He walked to Peterloo.[1] Oh yes! under the Saddleworth banner. Oh yes.) It tells you all about who was paid and how much they paid a week. All the money that they sent by stage-coach down to other areas like Kidderminster and down to Stroud. Oh yes! (I've been down to Stroud to see about that). It was when they had a turn-out, a lock-out, a strike or what, they sent money down. £5 was an enormous lot of money in those days. They sent it down by stage-coach.

'George Rhodes was a Chartist. He was a contemporary of Harney of Tiverton and Fielden of Todmorden and O'Connor who was the editor of the *Morning Star*. Rhodes was well thought of, and he was in favour of all the eight points of the Charter except one, and that was Suffrage at twenty-one. His letter on this to the *Morning Star* was really a classic. It was about people taking notice of a man of scruples, and what they should do when a man of principle and integrity and scruples said what he had to say. He was on about the youth of the day who were not mindful of events for the well-being of the community but were too bent on bear-baiting or the dog-fight or the pigeon-flying—and he related all the kinds of sport of the day. All this came down in the family. But for a lot of the family he was a kind of Red agitator: you'd call him a Marxist today. He was a tough egg.

'You ask me if there's any incident in my life I particularly remember. Oh, good gracious, yes! I remember one that has had the most lasting influence on my life, in a way. It was this. In 1911 there was a railway strike. And I'd paid a five shillings deposit on

---

[1] 1819: the dispersal of a sixty- to a hundred-thousand demonstration of people by the militia, an action that ended in the notorious massacre. See E. P. Thompson, *The Making of the English Working Class*, London, 1968, *passim*.

a week's holiday camp at Little Orme, Llandudno, and I was to go with my pal. The strike was declared on the Friday night so we couldn't go on the Saturday. The week cost £1, and we had paid five shillings deposit. The lads of the village—at least that side of the village—were older than us two and they went on bicycles, so there was no problem for them. They were going on bicycles anyway. We couldn't endure on the Saturday because we'd saved up this five bob and sent the deposit. I said to my pal (he's just died in recent months: I go to see them mostly once a month; they lived in a cottage adjacent to us when I was a little boy; there's still two of the family left), I said:

"Why don't we walk?"

"It's over a hundred miles!"

"So what!" I said. "Of course we can't lose five bob."

'So on the Sunday morning we set off. We set off with sandwiches and, I remember for some reason or other, a clean collar and a bathing costume in a piece of brown paper with a string on it. We walked and marched on this August morning down—oh, through my old constituency to Manchester. We were on Piccadilly steps; and there's a lavatory there, and my friend was fainting. So I took him down and put his head under the tap and pulled him round. And by this time we'd eaten all our food and we set off again.

'Now in those days there were no tarmac roads: they were all dust—water and sand bound. They had macadam, but it wasn't tarred macadam. And although there were only a few cars on the road, there were enough to stir it up. We'd been walking for forty-five miles when we got to a place called Kelsal Hill near Chester. By this time it was seven o'clock, and the sun was down and we were going mechanically then with blisters on our feet— but we couldn't stop. Just then the chapel *loosed* (I still go down through the village every now and again: I shall probably do it on Friday when I go to Chester). And a man walked alongside us and he said:

"How far have you come?" So we told him. He said:

"Good gracious!" he said. "That's nearly fifty miles!" We said, "Yes," and he said: "Ah well, perhaps you'll come in here for a bit."

'He opened the garden gate and we went down a path with old-fashioned flowers on either side. A woman came to the door and he said:

"I've brought two lads, and I'm telling them to go in the yard and have a wash. They can take all their clothes off and we won't look!"

'So we took all our clothes off and battered them and got the dust out of them as best we could. And then we went under the pump. By that time it was dark, and we presented ourselves at this back door; and he said, "Come in." And we had roast beef and ginger beer—and my word! didn't we eat a lot! Then he said:

"And what are you going to do?" (with a twinkle in his eye).

"Well," we said, "how much will it be?"

'He said: "Perhaps we can talk about that tomorrow."

"Oh no," we said, "we'll have to be going now, won't we?"

"No, I don't think so," he said, "except upstairs to bed!"

'We went upstairs to bed; and he sent us off in the morning. That was Monday morning, and by the time we got to Chester the strike was settled. And it cost us more to get from Chester to Llandudno and back home than it would have done from home to —but that didn't matter! We'd done the trick: we'd arrived. We'd set off: we'd done what we intended to do. And I must say, we were more comfortable on our backs swimming than we were walking about for the rest of that week.

'That was very memorable. And if every now and again I see anybody tramping through the village it makes all the difference. I think it shaped my life more than anything. And when Hitler's time came, and war was inevitable, my wife and I were sorry we were unable to do anything about it, unless that was something practical. So we adopted a Jewish German girl just before the war, and she's grown up as one of our own. That is the sort of influence that quite an innocent experience like that can very often produce.

'I had a lot of energy, and that is how I got my business going. I was a good singer, too. At least, I was sure I would have been a professional singer if I hadn't been wounded. When I was wounded it so tightened me up nervous-wise that it tightened my voice up; and it wasn't until middle age that my voice really became good again. (I have a good voice now: in fact just before Christmas I was asked by our mixed-voice choir at home to sing one of the Lancashire poems—Edwin Waugh's poems—accompanied by them; and it is going to be sold as a record for the coming Festival at Saddleworth. I'm singing *When the Sun Goes Down*.) Then after we got married I was interested in operatics; and eventually I got a company going and I used to produce opera and conduct it for some years—nearly ten years. I did this, and I got it on to the stage in the Grand Theatre in Oldham. I used to do a popular one of music hall and grand opera. That's what I'm keen on now.

'Then I decided I would go for local politics; and I was chairman of the council during the war. Then I went to Parliament for nineteen years. I'm a Freeman of the Borough where I live, and of my old constituency.

'There's a lot in continuity, but there's a lot in good fortune. I thank God every day that I'm able to do what I do. People rely on me a lot round where I live. There's hardly a week-end goes by unless somebody comes to the door. My wife says I'm the unofficial Ombudsman for all around this area.'

Apart from the intrinsic interest and the historical value that is in Lord Rhodes's story, it demonstrates very clearly the importance of the work tradition for the collector of social history from oral sources. For it is clear that the remarkable depth of the tradition in the Rhodes family is partly—perhaps chiefly—due to the continuity in the work. The family had kept up their tradition of hand-loom weaving for centuries: the skills were handed down from father to eldest son, and the family was tenacious of the reputation it had acquired for the quality of its cloth. The work itself consequently became the durable warp through which the weft of family and local history was richly and firmly interwoven. Undoubtedly, too, the long pedigree of the Rhodes family was closely tied up with the handing down of the craft skills from fathers to sons. It was not primarily a matter of genealogical pride but an attestation that the inherited skills had a long and unimpaired line. In this way it was analogous to the long and very ancient pedigrees that were preserved through patronymics in the Celtic countries. The Welsh pedigrees, for example, were not in their origin claims to any particular distinction in blood but the socially recognizable oral title to something tangible: the use of certain lands, for instance, or the right or obligation to maintain a certain office or craft within a family line.

2

Change in the Town

———————————— ✳ ————————————

Changes have been immense in town and country, and in both one of the most powerful agents has been the same—the self-propelled vehicle. The electric tram-car and later the motor-car altered the whole conception of the town or city. Instead of a community structured by walking-, horse transport- and cycling-distances, it was now possible for it to be expanded spectacularly to embrace a much wider area. This altered its basic character. Oral evidence from the people who remember the town or city before this expansion, much of it relating to the 1890s, can help to construct a vivid picture by including small details that have seldom been documented.

Here are some of the inhabitants of Ipswich recalling[1] town streets during the first decade of this century and the closing years of the last. Harry Wilton (born 1887) recalled:

'There were very few motor-cars about then [pre-1914] in comparison. There were bicycles certainly, but still plenty of horses. Even the carriages were still being used, especially for a funeral. It was most interesting to see a funeral then, with the horses going steadily along, possibly trotting back afterwards. Later, one of the most interesting things I saw was in the 1914–18 war when they came along and commandeered horses from the carts that were in the streets. I remember on one occasion the military took the horse away and left the man and his cart in the street. How he got his cart away I don't know. Horses, of course, were commandeered all over the place. The state of the streets? Of course you had your cleaners—street sweepers who were on the go nearly all the time. But horse manure, you must remember, had a value then; and the value increased with the decreasing number of horses in the streets. I recall one old man:

[1] George Ewart Evans, *Change in the Town*, BBC Third Programme, 8 April 1966.

31

I saw him come along with a pail: he was after some recent droppings; and he muttered:
"Gold dust! Gold dust!" '

Frank Wake (born *c*. 1888), who came into Ipswich as a boy of fourteen from the country, recollects the town streets:
'Oh, the roads—my goodness! We always used to laugh and say they put the granite down in the summer and scraped it up as mud in the winter. But the centre of the town was noted for the wooden blocks: they were quite good. That was paved with wooden blocks and that was quite good, but otherwise it was all mud in the winter. We had a tremendous lot of unemployed. They used to break granite, so much a bushel. And as I was working in the Town Hall I used to go down and measure it for them. You'd find some of them, they used to put wet clay at the bottom of a bushel, so half of it was stuck to the bottom when they emptied it. They were all right in those days! The drainage? I often wonder how the sewers got in because they weren't there when I came to Ipswich. Everybody had a pail, you see. During the night you used to stand them outside for the carts to come along and empty them. Night-soil they called it. The streets did smell; but nobody worried about smells then!'
An older inhabitant, Charles Chaplin (born 1883), remembered when the town was all alive with the horse-artillery clanking up and down with their spurs, and when everybody seemed to know one another:
'All them beautiful horses up there; see them come out; see them: eight horses on the gun when they was exercising on the heath. There were eight: eight bays, eight blacks, eight greys—we call them *greys*, but some people call them white. The blokes were sitting on them, and then there were others riding aside on them. When they went away at 10 o'clock all the chains shined like silver, and the horses' coats shined like silver. But you want to see them when they come home! The shine was all lathered; the horses were all of a sweat. They'd been all over the heath. Lovely to see them!'
Charles Chaplin was a carter for most of his life; and he recorded one of his earlier jobs in the town. He carted timber to the town jail.

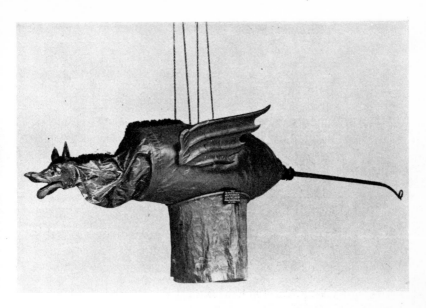

1 *Snap,* the Norwich Ceremonial Dragon. Model now in the Castle Museum, Norwich

2 W. R. Ward with a brougham, Aldeburgh (*c.* 1910)

3 W. R. Ward with the station bus, Aldeburgh

4 Southwold citizens: longshore fishermen (*c.* 1900)

'I carted wood in there for them to saw up; and I carted it out when it was sawed up. An old man by the name of Martin Krans, he was the bloke what supplied them with baulks of wood to cut up; and he took the wood away when it was done. And I'll tell you another thing: there's a lot of people never seen a treadmill where they sawed the wood up. A treadmill! And the prisoners were on it sawing up the wood.'

Cyril Angell (born 1898) remembers the first motor-cars in the town. They were regarded at that time as something of a joke; but, as we all know, they have taken a terrible revenge since:

'Well, in my boyhood days it was a most unusual thing to see a motor-car. Only a doctor here and there would have one. But I do remember on one occasion when we were going to a Sunday School treat, and were all walking along the road towards a park where we were to have our tea, that this builder who had a motor-car was trying to get up a hill. We were able to walk past him, much to our delight. But needless to say, he caught up with us later on, on the straight.'

Mrs Gwendoline Hancock (born 1899) describes the streets of the nearby town of Manningtree when she was a young girl:

'The type of traffic we saw then was the horse-drawn traffic, a carriage or two, the old *timberdy jig*, as we called it, on which we used to sneak a ride on the out-jutting bar of wood at the back; until somebody would call out: "Whip behind!" and of course we'd tumble in the dust to escape the carter's whip. Luckily for us there were no fast motor-cars. Yes, we'd find the old water-cart would be out on a summer's day. It was a fine lark that was, to run behind—against orders. But we were more or less always without our shoes and stockings in that area during the summer; always in and out of the water, in the river. And the driver of this water-cart could control the spray, that jutted forth from the back, by a lever at his side. And often he'd—I think quite often he would give it a pretty heavy press down; and we'd get soaked—much more than legs or feet!'

Cyril Angell describes the market day:

'Well, people came in from miles around; some with their horses and traps, and others in the carriers' carts. The cattle were driven in, generally walking, or they might come in with a horse-drawn vehicle. But more often than not they were driven in; and it was a busy day for everybody, including the shops, the businesses, the public houses. Everywhere else really came to life on the Tuesday, the market day. The ordinary small-holder as well as the bigger farmers brought in his produce. Butter and eggs were carefully packed on the Monday ready to come to be sold to the shopkeepers on the Tuesday. It was a strange experience sitting in a carrier's cart. You sat inside in the semi-darkness on a plank across the middle, as a rule; and you jolted along feeling every jolt in the road. It was a most unpleasant experience.'

But the effect of the motor-car on market day, as cars became more common, was most dramatic. The farmers when they travelled into market in their horse and traps tended to make a full leisurely day of it. When they got motor-cars they finished their business more quickly and returned home earlier. The inn-keepers noticed the difference: two daughters of Mrs Emma Wright (born 1870) of *The Water Lily*, Ipswich, underlined the difference:

'Oh yes, that has definitely altered now to what it used to be. The people have got the cars now so that they go back quicker than they used to, when they used to stop with the old carts and that. That used to take longer to do then with the carts than with the cars. In the old days we used to be up early; never in bed at 6 o'clock, always up. And we wouldn't finish until midnight, sometimes 1 or 2 o'clock in the morning. We were open from early morning till 11 o'clock at night. We used to do breakfast and lunches, cheese lunches, you see, for the farmers on a Tuesday. We used to cut off big chunks of bread and cheese, and put pickles on the counter for threepence a head. Father used to go out and get a big chunk of cheese on Tuesday mornings; and we used to do the cutting up, all ready; fill the table right full before they came in at 11 o'clock. Of course, my father was a good sportsman; and they all came to see him, and he used to have a little gamble with them and one thing and another. He kept them all together. Oh, it was a wonderful time really.'

These are just small vignettes, word pictures that cannot for a moment be considered as weighty historical evidence; but this is the kind of information that gives colour to bare fact or cold statistic. So also does a small incident related by Mrs Jessie Bussey who was born in 1897 in Norwich. It concerns *Snap*, the effigy of a dragon or monster, now in the Castle Museum, Norwich (Plate 1).

Every year it was processed round the city streets, originally under the powerful medieval *Guild of St George* who demanded a dragon as appropriate background in the annual *Riding of the Mayor*. This was a procession held on the Tuesday before Midsummer Day, nominally to mark the Mayor's being sworn into office, but in fact *ad maiorem urbis gloriam*. The Guild declined after the Reformation; and in 1731 it sold all its effects to the city, including 'One New Dragon, commonly called the Snapdragon'. Its value was three guineas.[1]

But Mrs Bussey depicts the dragon in his 'active' life; and this is the kind of function that oral evidence fulfils so well:

'I remember the incident very well. I have never forgotten it. I was terrified! When *Snap* came round in the yearly procession, we were all on the road watching. I think I must have—whether I thought I ought to go home—I can't remember that; but, anyhow, suddenly as I was running along, *Snap* snatched a red tam-o'-shanter cap off my head and put it—of course it dropped on the ground. Well, I screamed! and I suppose I picked it up. I went running home to my mother. I really was terrified! I was six or seven; about 1905 it would be.

'*Snap*, it has more or less of a dragon's head. It would be like a dragon with a big body, with bits hanging down so that a man could get inside. And he could see where he was going. Of course, I expect I thought the thing was alive. But it's still hanging in the Norwich Castle Museum, because I went there to a social not long ago with a friend and I saw it. And I said to her—she didn't know me when I was young:

"That thing once snatched my *tam* off my head!"

'And I never forgot it. I suppose he could manipulate the mouth, you see. I don't remember anything else that happened that day; the last thing I remember was running home because I was so frightened. I can't really remember what time of the year it was. But, as I say, I don't think it could have been winter because I had no coat on. I had a frock and a pinafore. In those days we used to wear white pinafores over our dresses, starched pinafores and they used to be like snow. My mother—she was most particular. All the girls had them; it was more or less a uniform I think. Black stockings and button boots.'

[1] Sylvia Haymon, *Norwich*, London, 1973, pp. 65–6.

The Town

A conversation with a native of the small Suffolk town of Bungay illustrates how the minutiae of change can be documented and given an exact date, the kind of change that happens almost insensibly; that is initiated perhaps by an individual, then followed by others and then forgotten as being too trivial to record. But, as in the present example, the small changes only serve to confirm how widespread was the revolution caused in town and country by the First World War, extending from the more obvious changes in transport and production to the more subtle changes in attitudes and dress. Isaac William Barber (born 1894) belongs to a family that has lived for many generations in the town of Bungay: he noticed the changes in the years immediately following his return from serving in the Navy:

'I think as regards people, I think they altered a good bit after the First War. I remember a fellow who is still alive: he'd got a baby son, and one Sunday morning he came along pushing it in a pram. People were outside talking to one another, and they saw him going down the street:

"Look! Here comes a man pushing a pram. Look!"

'They knew who it was; and it was something unusual to see a man pushing a pram. Of course, it took on afterwards; but previous to that you'd find the mother pushing the pram. You'd hardly ever see a man with her—not among the working class. But as I saw it, in some cases the man would be with her, but he wouldn't be pushing the pram; the woman had to push it. They thought that was the woman's job. She'd got the baby and she'd got to look after it and push it about. That's how it seemed.

'But I never saw many men about—not Sunday afternoons. I think they used to sleep mostly on Sunday afternoons because they were toiling all the week, you see. It'd be late before they got home at night, and they felt that Sunday was a rest-day, and they'd sleep in the afternoon. During the week, they'd be up early in the morning, some on 'em at 5 o'clock to be out to work—many of them—and it was 6 o'clock in the evening before they knocked off. At the printing works [in Bungay] they were going from 8 o'clock in the morning to 7 o'clock at night. That was the working day; fifty-four hours a week. When the old silk factory (Grout's) used to be going over at Ditchingham—my mother used to work there —they used to go to work at 6 o'clock in the morning till 6 o'clock at night for half a crown a week! That's true. That was a silk and crêpe factory, something to do with Norwich at that time o' day. The place is still there: it's a maltings now. That was the conditions, and some of 'em used to walk right from Three Ashes. My mother and an aunt used to walk from there—that's a mile and a half out of Bungay—walk all that way, night and morning for half a crown a week. The forewoman got 7s 6d. There used to be between 300 and 400 girls work there, I heard my father say.'

It is worth noting that there is no one now alive in the town who worked in Grout's silk mill, but there are a number of families where there are memories of the time when it was in full operation. Mrs Charles Fisher of Wainford, now in her eighties, recalls that her mother worked there. She told Mrs Fisher that when she went there she was so small that she had to have a box to stand on when she was at the loom. She often used to be sent out to buy a ha'porth of snuff for the women. There are also other traces of the silk mill. One of the oldest businesses in the town— S. N. Balls, ironmongers—still has, as part of the old stock, some of the square-toed clogs that were supplied to the girls working in the silk mills.

William Barber recorded an additional note about headgear and clothing in the town of Bungay:

'That was a friend of mine, just after the First War—he had a lovely head of hair, curly; and he came up the street one spring morning with no hat on. Well, we'd arranged to meet, about seven or eight of us and take perhaps a six- or seven-mile walk (if we went round Homersfield we'd go about nine miles: we used to walk a lot). He'd got—he did have a brain operation, you see; he was shot about during the war, a very tricky operation. Of course, we thought he'd gone a bit mental because he'd got no hat on. No one had ever gone without a hat: everybody put on their caps or trilby or velour—mostly velour then—or straw hats.

"What's wrong, Harry?"

"What do you mean?"

"Haven't you got your hat?"

"I don't want a hat. I've already got a hat. Nature's hat!"

'He had a lovely head of hair. Well, it weren't long before that copped on. He was the first one in Bungay. That would be about 1919, that was. He was the first one with no hat. And then of all the funny things—there was a very hot summer, 1921. Well, someone said:

"Well, I ain't going to put my waistcoat on this afternoon."

'He went just like we do now. But then we always had a waist-coat with a suit, summer and winter. And I remember I come down the street—we all after a time, we all left them off: of course, you had your hands in your pockets showing your white shirt:

"Look at them crazy b's. They ain't got no waistcoats on! They must be a-going loopy!"'

William Barber also illustrates how valuable family tradition is in supplementing the history of a town. He worked for most of his life in Richard Clay's (The Chaucer Press) printing works, operating a book-binding machine. He is a great reader, has a retentive memory, and has always been sensitive to traces of the town's history. He had a very early training in this:

'My grandmother, when I was a child, she used to take me round and show me the historical facts of things, and point out different things of interest. I was about seven or eight years of age. She was born somewhere about 1844; perhaps before, because my grandfather helped to build the railway, and that started about 1854. So she must have been born about the 1830s. One day she took me on to Outney Common; then she said:

"This is the place, during the Plague of 1665 where they buried about 300 people who had died through the plague."

'There was a pest-house built—I don't know what period it was built, anyhow it was taken down in 1774 and sold for £40. She said 300 people were buried there. It's now somewhere near the Number Two green on the Common. And to confirm what she said, I'll think you'll find it in one of Sir Rider Haggard's books. He states that several of those who died from the plague were buried on Bungay Common, "now sacred to a golf-green", that's how he put it. And my grandmother pointed out to me where it was. The green is like this [a slight hollow] where the earth is sunk down. She said 300: it may have been 340: she just said 300. That's what she told me then.

'Then she took me round to different places like St Mary's churchyard where her forebears were buried. They were named Redgrave, and they've got stones up; there's a lot of stones there. There's my Uncle Ned, and various other people. And she pointed out to me where John Barber Scott was buried. He died in 1867. But he was a great man in the town, a great benefactor. In fact, he lent the money to pebble-stone the streets, which you'll still see in some of them now. They've been covered up where the old Butter Cross is: the gulley-ways were all pebbled to drain the water away. He was a well-known man. He met Napoleon—I think it was at Elba. My grandmother knew John Barber Scott. There used to be a school in Broad Street, called the Old School Room now, just along by the Theatre; and there used to be one in Outney Road towards the Common—a National School. But when it was holiday time, my grandmother she used to take kiddies in to get them off the street, you know, because they used to have big families then. And this John Barber Scott wanted her to be a school-teacher. I suppose he had influence: he was one of the heads; and he walked with her, oh! a long way, persuading her to be a school-teacher. But she wouldn't accept. She was a very intelligent sort of person, although she never had the education, more or less self-taught. Of course, a lot of them didn't go to school at that time o' day. Kiddies used to be at work, nine or ten years of age, in the field. They were bread-winners.

'And she told me certain things about the stealing that went on in order to live. In many places—oh, they would steal things, rob hen-roosts. She remembered when they used to be hung for sheep-stealing. Her—that would be her brother-in-law, that would be my grandfather's brother—he stole a purse, she told me, and he was transported to Botany Bay, for stealing a purse with seven-and-six in it. But the funny thing about it was that the family—they were all great, strong healthy children. There were nineteen children. Three of them in the Life Guards were six foot three. My father told me there was one named Ruth (my grandmother had told me this but I'd forgotten about it); they were all named from the Bible; that was the tradition. My name is Isaac William. There was Abraham, Jacob, Ruth, Rebecca, Jemima, Eliza: that was my grandfather's family. They were tree-fellers on my father's side; and Ruth used to go in the woods, and cut down trees with them. My father said they just lived on bread and swede. And the grocer that owned the house what they lived in, a grocer named Moore, he has told me about all this:

"Your father and grandfather and great-grandfather," he said, "were the finest physical men who ever lived in Bungay."

And he told me all about them. One of them—that would be the great-grandfather—he was a tree-feller, lifted a donkey and cart up. He used to take the donkey and cart into the woods to

cut down trees, his wife with him. And he said—an old pub called
The Thatched House which is not in being now; that's where the
farmers used to get—and they made a bet (he, my great-grandfather, didn't have any money); they wagered £5 that he'd lift the
donkey and cart. They'd all got to be off the ground at once. And
I questioned that; so he said:

"Well, he took the donkey out of the cart; threw the donkey;
tied it up with the ropes he used for putting on the trees; lifted the
donkey onto the cart; put the harness in (he say: 'You can have
the harness and all!') got underneath and lifted it up like that!"

'That's what Mr Moore told me; and I asked my father if it was
correct, and he said:

"Yes, who told you that?"

'My great-grandfather and his wife lived near where Jermy's
shop is. This used to be a baker's shop; it used to be Ecclestone's.
Well, they brought a load of flour: in fact, they used to have sacks
of flour then of twenty stones. Twenty stones! What a weight!
And she had to come up to the top of this lane: she lived just
round the corner:

"Oh!" she said. "I could do with a sack of that flour in my
house!"

'Of course, the feller who was in charge said:

"If you can carry one, Ma'am, you can have it!"

'Well, she got it onto her back and took it indoors. And he:

"Oh, I didn't mean you to have that, Ma'am," he said. (My
father told me this); she got the chopper up:

"Don't you come in my house. Do, I'll chop your head off.
You said I could have it, and I'm a-going to keep it!"

'He had to clear off. Whatever he done, I don't know. I heard
that from my grandmother as well. It was quite correct.

'But in this place there was only one room downstairs; and two
bedrooms. There was a big room, little old lean-to place. They
brought nineteen children up in there. But there wasn't nineteen
children all the time, of course; they'd be gone away. As I said,
there was one of the family, her name was Ruth. And Wombwell's
Menagerie come to Bungay; and it was in St John's Road. And
young Wombwell asked for volunteers to go into the lions' den
with him. And this young girl—I heard this Mr Moore and my
father say so—she was one of the finest specimens of woman you
ever saw: a great fine girl. She was about seventeen; and she volun-

teered to go in with the lions. And young Wombwell was so struck with her bravery and physical condition that he married her. She became a Mrs Wombwell. And she had been over to Bungay since—which I didn't know. I'd liked to have seen her because she was getting into years then—they all lived old, a very old age! She was somewhere getting onto ninety when she came to Bungay. But I think they settled in Newcastle. They had a lot of property there.'

Another example of the usefulness of family memories in giving an extra dimension to a town's history comes from Ipswich. Robert G. Pratt (born 1910), a tailor, talked about his grandfather who came down from Scotland in the nineteenth century and founded the business:

'My grandfather first worked with a grocer. He was very good at this trade of grocer, and he saw an opportunity which existed at that time, particularly in the sale of tea. Tea was a commodity rather confined to the gentry because they had to take delivery by the chest; which meant it was quite outside the scope of the village and cottage dweller: they couldn't buy tea. The only chance they ever had of tasting a cup of tea was to get somebody on the staff of one of the big houses to surreptitiously take a little from a caddy. So my grandfather, seeing that the poorer classes could benefit by a cup of tea, decided that he would start blending his tea to suit the water and carry it on his back. Remember, tea is very light: you can carry quite a quantity in a pack. So he became a packman, and he travelled the villages round about Ipswich with this pack of tea on his back; and he made it up into little packages and sold it to the cottage folk.

'Well now, he must have been very successful with this until the time came when the big concerns started selling packed teas; and this did rather affect his trade. But being a go-ahead Scotsman, he wasn't going to be put off by that. He had by that time bought himself a pony and trap; and he—by a rather strange way, I suppose—came to sell clothes. No doubt somebody who he was selling his tea to had said that they wanted something from the town in the way of a suit for their son, Jimmy; and he said: "Right, well I'll bring you one." No opportunity lost you see! And from that he built up quite an extensive business in clothing. By virtue of his weekly and monthly calls he could take money for these clothes by instalments; and that really is how the present [clothier's] business came to begin.

'I don't know how many ponies and traps he had all over the county of Suffolk, but it was quite a considerable number. And he did succeed to the extent of becoming a town councillor for Ipswich. On this council he earned himself the nickname of *More Light Pratt*. Now the way that came about was this: Ipswich was poorly lit, as probably were most towns of the period; and he felt that electricity, being something new, had possibly great advantages to offer. He had to make his calls for his payments in some very dark alleys and courts where there was no light whatever; and he knew perhaps better than most what went on in these dark back roads. He studied the possibility of getting electricity to the town and he persuaded the council to let him travel up to Glasgow to report on the system that was operating there. He reported back and managed to persuade the town council of the benefits that would come from the new source of power. As a result Ipswich got its electrical undertaking and finally got its trams.'

3
Changes in Business Methods

———————— ✳ ————————

We tend to link the changes of this century, both in town and country, with the improvement of communication, the mechanization of transport and—especially—of the old hand-processes. Equally important changes were going on elsewhere, and these tend to be taken for granted. But oral evidence can offer us particular and sometimes surprising information about one sector or other, for instance, business methods. In this short chapter we gather that the rhythm and technique of business in at least one provincial town were still basically those of the nineteenth century even until well after the First World War. An informant gives us a glimpse of the working of a provincial bank, a branch of one of the big banks, in the mid-twenties: for various reasons he prefers to withhold his name:

'In 1922 I left the grammar school in my home town to join a branch of the old "London and Provincial Bank", in a town some distance away. I was only a junior, of course; and by the time I began the "London and Provincial" had become a subsidiary of Barclays. The staff of the bank—I am not quite sure—was approximately nine or ten, of which I was the junior, responsible for stamp-licking and odds and etcetera. One of the strange things I remember is at that time the manager was doing all his own correspondence in long hand in copying ink; and I had to take a duplicate of the letters in a damp-leafed book which would give the index for reference purposes before the letter was sent to the customer. Typists for us were unknown.

'Another thing is that they were very bad times for small farmers; probably—but I'm not going to stick my neck out too far—good times for the big farmers. But in spite of all the money troubles that the farmers were faced with, to me—it seemed to me that they were a far nicer people to deal with than people today. Inasmuch as any of the bank-staff could visit almost any farmer who traded (perhaps I should say banked) with us, at any time and would be made welcome, and could gather fruit when it was in season. And on market day when we kept open until 4 p.m., an hour beyond the normal time, at the close of the day there would be a heap behind the counter: of pheasants, rabbits and so on brought in by the farmers—in spite of the hard times. Also, a very interesting point to me, is how much we have declined in public morality (I think that's the word I should use) from those days. At that time, when the manager wanted to go away for a few days' holiday or a week-end or even a month, I as junior clerk had to sleep on the premises—in charge. I was the security department! My armament consisted of one three-foot ebony ruler which we used in the course of our duties; and which I carried when I went round and inspected the windows before retiring to the manager's flat above to pass the night.

'I was never asked if it was convenient for me to do these duties. I was simply told that the manager was going off, therefore it was my job. I was never paid. My remuneration was 2s 6d for a break-fast allowance. I wonder how many bank officials would do it today. I wouldn't like to commit myself on the amount of wage I was getting. But my salary was probably not more than £8 or £9 a month; but I'm not sure. But there was no overtime—of that you may be sure!

'But there's another aspect of banking I didn't like at that period. That was the method of half-yearly charging for keeping cus-tomers' accounts: it literally amounted to the more you had the more you got. In other words, the small farmer, working on a small overdraft and probably one or two cheques *R.D'd* in the course of six months, was not very popular. And he could get stuck with charges of five guineas on top of his interest; and the big customer who had a nice floating credit-balance could get away with a guinea for using six or seven pages on a ledger. So there was no rhyme nor reason because the charges were a matter for the manager. They were nothing to do with the bank. Now this is the kind of stamp that we put on:

Int	£
Charges	£
	————
Total	

'You stamped that on at the end of the half-year. The top is the interest which was worked out. The ledgers I took into the manager's office, as junior; and the pages were turned to the customer's name; and the manager would say what the charges were to be, and then you made the total. And a big account would in some cases even get one percent on his current account as well as interest on his deposit.

'Apart from that, which I didn't think was very business-like, the manager used to attend the cattle-market: in these days the manager ran the insurance side of a company; and the manager took the whole of the commission. I think present-day practice is that the bank and the manager share the commission between them. In those days the manager took the lot. The manager would meet the farmers in the ring when they bought; and he would say:

"Now, Joe, don't you think you'd better get that beast insured?"

'That was the principle of the thing. And the manager always sat in his office which faced the main door so that when the customers arrived on market day he would shout out to the right man:

"Good morning, George. Good morning, Jack. Come inside!"

'And there was a welcome at the door, and [raises his elbow] for the right ones.

'Well now, I would like to just tell you two incidents in connection with the market. We had one man that couldn't even write: he could only sign with a cross. He used to come in before he went to the cattle-ring to see if he could afford to buy a beast. He could have gone and bought the whole market! But he had to be sure he had the money. We had another customer that used to come just on 4 o'clock, closing time, to count his balance from the ledger. It was placed in a japanned deed-box, put on the side of the counter. When he came in he went up to the end, and opened it; brought out his notebook; added up what he'd paid in, what he paid out; balanced it up; then he carefully went through it, and put it back in the deed-box and said: "Yes, that's right!" He was satisfied his money was still there. He wasn't a small farmer: he was in quite a nice way. Well, I wouldn't like to say—probably with 500 or 600 quid which was quite a reasonable amount in those days. But he had always to count to see his money was safe. I believe he thought the deed-box was where his money came out of.

'And referring to commission. I do know that the manager at

one time managed to buy himself a new car out of his commission on *one* life-insurance. I think it was for a £10,000 life-insurance. And it was for the life of a gentleman farmer. I know the manager bought this new car; and it was said he earned more on his insurance commission than he got in bank salary. And of course, a lot of the insurance was done by debit-slips; that is to say, we held the accounts so we didn't have to get the customer to come in to pay his insurance. With the debit-slips all we had to do was to make out a debit-slip of the two guineas, three guineas, whatever it was, and pass it through. So the bank staff did the work for the insurance company, and the bank manager drew the full commission.

'But after a period in the bank I had an illness; and I couldn't settle. I don't think I was much use to them, and I don't think they were much use to me! I had too much of a gypsy in the blood, I suppose. Anyway, I left the bank.'

4

A Town Horseman

———————————— * ————————————

I recorded William R. Ward of Aldeburgh in August 1968, and
again in March 1975. He was born in 1878 and spent most of his
life in this Suffolk town. The whole of the account he gave me
demonstrates the ability of the men of his generation to tell an
interesting story. He had grown up and lived for the most of his
life in a predominantly oral culture, when a man gained social
acclaim from his skill in narration; for telling a story—either at
work or at leisure, in the street or the public house—was one of
the ways in which a man who had the gift could fulfil himself and
at the same time amuse his fellows.

William Ward spent most of his working life, certainly the
formative part of it, in horse-transport; and later he was compelled to change over to motor-buses. He describes his work
chiefly against the background of late-Victorian and Edwardian
Aldeburgh, at that time a highly fashionable watering-place. Once
again, these recordings are a good example of a man describing his
lifetime's work and its social context with a detail whose accuracy
cannot be faulted.

'I shall be ninety the 3 October [1968], in two months' time. I
was born in Aldeburgh, not far away—just across the road. Yes,
and I lived in Aldeburgh all my working days really, except for a
few years I went besides Nottingham, during the last war. I was
at a Government depot there, Cherwell.

'In 1890 I left school and I was an errand boy for a grocer for
some time. Then I had a little spell as an errand boy at an iron-
monger's; but I found that the flavour of paraffin wasn't half so
nice as handling groceries. So I went with a man who had horses
and carriages to hire out; and I stayed with him all my working
days.

'I worked for twenty-nine years with horses; and I done a
lot o' time driving the horse-bus to the station. I wonder what

they'd say today if it came down Aldeburgh High Street! (Plate 3)
I was the man that drove the bus in 1900—that's when I started—
till 1922 when they turned it into a motor-bus.[1] I wrote a little
poem about it, too.[2] But I went to work for a jobbing master who
kept the *East Suffolk* [hotel] stables. He used to manage all kinds
of vehicles such as run to meet a train; and the visitors that came
to Aldeburgh used to hire these carriages to go out for drives and
take them to places like Dunwich, Orford, Sibton, Butley, Fram-
lingham—a lot of visitors were interested in old ruins, you see.
Mr Ward, the jobbing master, eventually opened the garage, as I
say, in 1922. But before he done that I used to drive people out
for drives, two-hour and three-hour drives; and we used to go
round the country: Snape, Butley, Blaxhall; we used to go to
Woodbridge, too. In the summer it was quite a business. There
was a good class of people come to Aldeburgh in them days, before
motors were invented.

'Well, they'd hire a carriage or a wagonette. They used to pay
about fifteen bob for the wagonette, for a day. You had to stop and
rest the horse for two hours, d'you see. It gave them time to look
round the ruins. Of course, if they had a carriage, it used to come
to about a guinea—a carriage with a pair of horses in it. But a
single-horse wagonette would be about fifteen bob; and the same
it used to be for Orford and them places, about twelve or thirteen
miles. The wagonette would carry five passengers and the driver;
and we had larger vehicles, you see, a wagonette that held seven
passengers and the driver. And then what they called a small
brake, that carried twelve people and a driver. We had other
vehicles besides: landaus, victorias, phaetons, dog-carts, gover-
ness-carts, broughams. Ward, the jobbing master, used to go up
to London and buy things like that. Always a lot o' stuff like that
would be sold up in London; and in the same way he used to buy
the horses up in London. These big London horse-auctioneers
would send him a programme when they were having something
extra—any extra horse being sold, like. I remember the Terra
Bona Tea Company went smash. There was about 500 horses
sold: of course Ward went up and bought a couple of them. Another time he told me:

"I got a programme—I got a catalogue from Ward's in the

---

[1] He was known in the town as *Busman Bill*.
[2] See Appendix, pp. 189–90.

5 The Southwold town crier: Mr Moore (*c.* 1890)

6 The Southwold lifeboat being drawn through the town: *The Rescue* (1908)

Edgware Road. There's a cab-company gone smash, and there are 400 horses going to be sold."

'So he used to go up and buy a horse or two, because we had fifteen horses in the summer; and we used to sell off three or four of them after the summer. We'd winter two or three of them on the meadows; have a big shed there so the horses could get in in rough weather. And then we used to feed them; take the bait down to them every day. As I said, he used to sell two or three and buy fresh ones in the spring. Well, of course, we runned into a bit of trouble one time when he went up to Ipswich and bought one. It was a very savage beast—but that's a long story. *Man-eater* we called him. One night I met the last train in with the bus; and done my horse up what I had on the bus; and then went to this *Man-eater* to do him up. Of course, I gave him a good rub down and brushed him down, chucked the rug over his back; went to feel round to get at the strap in the front—well, he got hold of my back and pushed me against the chest. I couldn't move! And as luck would have it, Ward came in, and he could see that he'd got hold of me. So he picked up a broom and gave it a couple of cracks o' the skull and made it drop me.

"Blast!" he says, "he's a rum 'un!"

'Of course, when it dashed to get hold of me it chucked the old staple out of the wall that it was fastened on, tied up to, you see. They were all right for quiet horses. But for this one, chucking round in a hurry, it wasn't no good for him. 'Course, next morning Ward went to the blacksmith to ask him to make an extra-long staple to go in the wall; he phoned up Saxmundham for a new headstall, and went to the blacksmith for about eighteen inches of chain, as much as to say:

"That's as much as you're going to have, Charlie!" So he took and fastened the old hobby up like that. But I tell you I had a narrow escape! I said to my wife when I got home that night:

"Cor! my owd back smart!"

'She said: "Oh?"

"An owd hoss got hold of my back."

'So she said: "Let's look at it."

'So I pulled up my shirt and vest, and she said:

"No wonder! There's a piece as big as your thumb out of your back!"

'I was lucky you know. If he'd ha' then got me, he'd ha' squeezed my ribs if owd Ward hadn't ha' come and give him a clop o' the skull with that broom. I was lucky! But that *Man-eater* he bit everybody in the stables: it didn't matter—everyone in the stable he drew blood out of. He was a vicious devil; and of course nobody was anxious to use the damned thing, on account of—well, when you put the collar over the head and the head come through, you might—you were looking out for your face, you see. Then he had a go at Ward himself. The old horse made a grab at his wrist when he let go of the headstall. He broke that vein in his wrist and the blood squirted out; and it wasn't long then before Ward said: "We'll get rid of him!" He went from us, and eventually he killed a man in Lowestoft; and the police followed his ownership back, and they were satisfied then that he should be destroyed. So that was the finish of *Man-eater*!

'But I went to Ward's in 1892 and I learned the business as I went along. I took a great interest in horses, and learned a lot. I got one or two good veterinary books, and I studied them so that I was really very clever with horses. I used to give a ball when it was needed; do the grinders when they needed rasping. The horse's teeth get sharp so they bite the inside of the mouth and make it sore, so they can't eat very well. And when they do that you had a long rasp and rasped the edges down. You could always tell whether you'd done the job decently: the old horse—they always left in the manger, there'd be all white marbles, the food where it's rumbled about. They weren't eating it. I got quite efficient at that sort of thing. Then after all that studying, the horses went away like snapping your finger! Horses went off away; and all I studied about horses was useless in the finish. I was pretty smart: I could ride and drive, you see.'

William Ward also recorded a number of stories that help to recapture the atmosphere both of his job and of the Aldeburgh scene before the First World War:

'An old gentleman he used to go to the golf a good bit; and if he was the only person in the vehicle he would talk to himself. This was a wagonette I was driving at the time. So he was close up behind me, a-sitting as I was driving. And hearing him talking to himself one morning as I was going along, I turned half-round and said:

"I beg your pardon, sir."

'He said: "It's all right, Ward; I was talking to myself," he said.

"But you are sure of two things when you talk to yourself: there's a good man talking; and the next is there's a good man listening."

'Doing the bus-work, you see, we used to go and pick up people for the early train. But it was not often: you had about one order for the early train. And one morning I went to pick up a man for the train; and I had an open carriage, a wagonette. The man was rather—making it rather late coming to the trap, to go to the station; and as he got in, his housekeeper came out with a bowl of hot soup and a spoon and handed it to him. We hadn't got far along the road going to the station when it started to snow very heavily. And I turned round and had a look, and saw the unusual sight of a man spooning a bowl of hot soup in a snowstorm!'

The following story gives a good picture of his working day and of his clientele:

'When I used to run a service with a bus to the golf-links, some of the golfers who used to come and get in the bus used to be rather fidgety about wanting to get off, and used often to say:

"Oh, it's time we were going, Ward!"

'Perhaps I'd look at my watch and say:

"Oh, it's a couple of minutes to go."

"Oh no!" they'd say, "the time is up!"

'But Sir John Baldwin, he always had the right time, and a little silver watch and no chain on; so he used to put his fingers in his waistcoat pocket and bring it out, and he'd say:

"You are right, Ward."

'Now one morning, Mr Paget who was rather fidgety, said:

"Time we were off, Ward! Time we were off, Ward!"

"Oh no, sir," I said, "a couple of minutes to go!"

'And I turned round and looked at Sir John Baldwin. He said to me:

"It's no good looking at me, Ward," he says, "I've left my watch under the pillow in a sleeping coach coming from Romania to Paris."

'So I said: "You've said good-bye to that then, sir."

"No, no, Ward," he said, "that attendant knows me as well as you do."

'Well, Sir John Baldwin used to go off every now and again on some commission for the Government, and a short while afterwards he went off again. And after he got back, it was on a Saturday

morning; and I went to the bus as it was waiting for the golfers
to come and get into. Sir John Baldwin was there: he was the
only one in the bus. As soon as I went to the bus he said:

"Good morning, Ward."

I said: "Morning, Sir John."

'And he just put his fingers in his waistcoat pocket and held out
his hand and said:

"My watch, Ward!"

'There ain't many people in this country could have done that,
is there? I thought that was really wonderful. He must have
treated them attendants some well to make them worry about
saving his watch!

'Another time when I was driving the wagonette to the golf-club
and I got Mr Willett and some of his friends in the vehicle. He
said to them, he said:

"Here I was lying in bed this morning," he said, "the sun
shining in here lovely at 6 o'clock. There I lay in bed wasting
time; and eventually we come up to the links at 10 o'clock. We
are half-way round about 11 o'clock, no shelter and it comes on to
rain; or else comes very dull. Mostly it's a shower of rain and no
shelter. If we'd got up an hour earlier we should have finished the
round and have been near the club-house for shelter."

'Those were the words, or practically the words, that he told his
friends: the very first morning it came into his mind. That was
Mr Willett who thought up Daylight Saving. And I remember—
because we used to drive some classy people about. I took Knollys
who used to be a great high-up in Queen Victoria's household. His
family come and stayed at the *Wentworth* some time, and I went;
took my horse and a Suffolk up and horsed the *Wentworth* bus;
and took them to the station. I driv them. One or two classy
people I've driven, you see.'

It may be asked: 'Are these anecdotes worth the oral historian's
attention?' I believe they are because both give the atmosphere of
the job and both underline the accuracy of an informant when he
is talking directly about it. These two stories show that William
Ward's memory was still accurate, even after a period of well over
sixty years. On going to the printed word I found that Viscount
Knollys was Gentleman Usher to Queen Victoria and, later,

A Town Horseman

Secretary to George V; and that Lieutenant-Colonel Sir John Baldwin was a diplomat and soldier who had a house in Aldeburgh. He was British Consul in Romania in 1912; and it is probable that it was in that year he lost his watch. The story about William Willett also illustrates the quality we often find in the narrative of ordinary people. They tend to dramatize events and shape them artistically, bringing them within the compass of their own experience, paying less regard to the extended background of the event which is beyond their ken. As already suggested, when a man speaks about the work he has been doing for most of his life you can rarely fault him. But when he relates events outside his own immediate experience, we have always to allow for this mythopœic quality which often discloses the narrator to be more of a poet than a chronicler. The legends of Newton and the apple, and Watt and the steaming kettle are of a similar character. But to be fair to William Ward, he claims only tentatively that the Daylight Saving Act arose directly out of the Aldeburgh experience and that it helped to bring the problem (probably not for the first time) and its possible solution to William Willett (1865–1915), the tireless advocate of the scheme who, nevertheless, did not survive to see it put into effect. I suspect that William Ward, as the poems in the Appendix show, would be prouder of the title of poet than anything else; and it is the poet in him that was undoubtedly uppermost when he recorded the following two stories:

'Now Hannah Ward, she was a person spent several years working in a gentleman's family; and the younger generation took an interest in her still, and used to pass on their clothes to Hannah. Hannah always went to church on Sunday mornings; and this particular Sunday morning she was dressed out in a lovely summer-frock and a big, broad-rimmed hat with a lot of ribbons round it—proper to keep the sun off, you know. And Hannah was going down the aisle as they were singing the first hymn: *Hallelulia! Bless the Lord*, when Hannah suddenly turned sharply round and walked out of church. But some lady who knew Hannah well, thought to herself: "What can be wrong with Hannah? She can't be ill; do, she wouldn't have come out so quickly." So after the church service she went down to Hannah's house and said to her:

"Whatever made you come out of church this morning, Hannah?"

53

"So would you come out if you'd been insulted!"

"Insulted! I don't understand you."

'So Hannah said:

"Oh, you may not but I do!" she said. "Weren't they singing: Hallelulia! Hallelulia! Hardly-knew-yer, Hannah Ward." '

The second story:

'I was driving a man from the golf-links, and as we went down the High Street, he said:

"Ing! Ing! That's a funny name!"

'It was the name over a shop. I said:

"Yes, and that's a funny way he got it!"

"How's that?"

"Well," I said, "years ago when they were giving out the names in Aldeburgh," I said, "when they come to the end of it, there was one name, and two people for one name: and the name was *Whiting*. So the people said to one of the men, they said:

"Well, you'll have to be Mr *White*," and to the other, "you'll have to be Mr *Ing*!"

"And that's how he come to get his name." '

'Yes, I wrote another poem about wild-fowling. I was friendly with a man who done a lot of wild-fowling; and he used to go round the river bank when it was moonlight and when the tide was coming in. Of course, he knew all about the river, and knew the places to look up, where there were no saltings—mud-flats where the birds used to come and settle and search for food. And he used to have a little pair of glasses so that he could tell whether there was birds at the water's edge; and then he used to wait until they—until the tide brought them in within gun's range. That's how I got to know about the wild-fowl and come to write the poem.'[1]

A man of William Ward's age and intelligence can be a valuable asset to the local historian: he can give him unusual and often valuable information about the town and the village; and sometimes he can uncover a stimulating clue or lead that could well put the student on an original line of research. For it is likely that a

[1] See Appendix.

great deal of the late nineteenth century is not recorded in print; and even if it is, the lead one gets through oral evidence considerably narrows down the search for any corroborating information that has already been documented. In my experience it is best not to be too specific, at least at first, in one's questions about an informant's early years, but to make the general, if rather clichéd, observation about the changes he has seen in his lifetime; and then to see what emerges. He is thus likely to get, as here, a good range of possible topics—one or more of which could be followed up, ideally on another occasion!

'When I was very young they started to build the pier at Aldeburgh; and it got well out into the sea when a ship got wrecked, and it washed off during the night and went right into the pier. My father said he didn't know whether it was their hearts or their pockets, but they never built the pier any more. But they took the part down that was furthest out to sea, and left the other part for quite a few years. And boys and men used to go on to the pier to fish. Of course, it must have reached a fair way into the sea for a big ship to float past it and wreck it. As a very small boy I used to go with my cousin who was six years older than me; and when he used to go fishing he used to take us boys with him. So I really went on the pier a few times; and I don't think anybody else in Aldeburgh now ever walked on the pier. They took the part down that was in the sea and left three or four piles standing on the beach; and the fancy brickwork that was going to be the entrance to the pier, they left that standing. The pier stood right opposite the Moot Hall. I could come down Church Hill and I could have went straight on to the pier. It was built of round, iron piles; and I can remember the cross-work that bound them together. I can remember that quite plain.

'But there were two things I heard said the day the lifeboat turned over. I was standing on the beach near the lifeboat watching the men putting on their belts and oilskins; and a cousin of mine was standing there; and her husband used to go with the lifeboat a good bit. And a woman came up and said to her:

"Is Bill in the boat?"

'She said: "No, but Bob is,"—that was her brother—"and I think that one of a family is enough in the boat today!"

'In less than half an hour the lifeboat had turned over and drowned six men. I thought that was very funny that she should say that. And the coxswain of the lifeboat, he was ill in bed when the rockets went up to summon the lifeboat crew; and he got up and dressed and came to the lifeboat and was putting on his belt when the doctor came and forbade him to go in it because he knew he didn't ought to be out of bed. But the coxswain he stood on the beach watching the boat get away, and he was talking to a man and he said:

"He ought to let go that *warp* now!"

'And he hadn't said the words hardly a minute when the lifeboat swung clear of the warp: which shows that the man in charge of the lifeboat, he knew his job, the same as the coxswain would have done. (The warp is a rope that goes out and is fastened to an anchor—well out at sea; and the warp was put on the bow of the lifeboat, and ran alongside. And the crew can pull on it and help to haul the boat away from the beach. When they get a certain distance, they drop the warp overboard and away the boat would go.) So I thought they were two unusual sayings; and I heard them, and nobody else in the place heard: but they stuck in my mind. But it was unlucky, that day. That was 1899. And that night I drove a pair of horses fifty-two miles: twenty-six miles up to Ipswich hospital and twenty-six miles back again, fifty-two miles. A woman, when she was told the lifeboat had capsized, the shock to her—she fell down and broke her leg. And that's why I had to drive up to Ipswich hospital, on the 7 December. So it wasn't a picnic!

'I've seen a good lot of changes: I've seen oxen ploughing in the fields, and I've seen an ox in a tumbril, working in the field. They were on the Redhouse Farm at Aldeburgh; but the ox I saw in the tumbril was at Aldringham: it belonged to the Ogilvies' estate. I've seen them; and I've seen oxen ploughing in the fields here. They had collars, not a yoke. That was in 1894, I seen a few freaks, too, in Aldeburgh. I seen a sheep with five legs walking in Aldeburgh; and I see a horse with five shoes on in Aldeburgh. I went into the blacksmith's shop with one of our horses, and the blacksmith called me forward. He said:

"Here, Bill! Something you won't see every day!"

'And he picked up one of the horse's feet, and it had got two hooves, and both of them were shod, so the horse had five shoes on. It belonged to a circus or something, and it was took to the blacksmith to be shod. That was a freak. When I was a small boy, the man who kept *The Cross* hotel had a pet turkey that used to run about the street just as it liked. Nobody took any notice of it, to try to hurt it or anything like that. So it used to run near *The Cross* like an old hen running about a farmyard. The boys—that was used to human beings and it didn't take any notice of them—the boys used to go up to it and say: *"Gobble, gobble, gobble!"*; and the old thing would say: *"Gobble, gobble, gobble!"* back, as much as to say: "I'll *gobble* you!"

'There used to be a *camera obscura* on Aldeburgh beach, too. I never went inside of it. But I used to go with the other boys and peep in. It's worked by mirrors, isn't it? Well, that's what it was: *a camera obscura*. Of course, we also had a *velocipedestriantricano-logist*. He rode a velocipede! There was also a concert party used to come to Aldeburgh and stay for a week. There was one of the men there, used to come: he used to have a *hydrodectoloptitric-harmonica*. It was just a great number of tumblers partly filled with water, and he'd get a tune out of them. But what I meant was, that on them bills this *hydrodecti*—and so on—was in big letters to draw attention. And the people thought they were going to see something wonderful!

'But lots of changes: the coastguard station used to be near the look-out. There used to be a flagstaff and a brass cannon: they fired that twice when the lifeboat crew was summoned. And there was the old pound used to be on the cricket-field where they used to put stray animals in that and kept them till they could find their owners. And there used to be three lime-kilns in Aldeburgh; and there were five mills in Aldeburgh: two draining mills and three corn mills, when I was quite a lad—I'm speaking about that time now. There really have been a lot of changes. There used to be a lovely pine wood in North Field; but they cut the trees down and moved them away to clear a space for the caravans. There was a lovely pine wood there. The Crag Path went as far as the village of Slaughden. Crabbe? I never heard of any stories about him. I've read his life and his poems: a book I lent to my grand-daughter. He didn't used to—how shall I put it?—he didn't use to praise the Borough up or yet the people, did he? But I'll tell you this: when I was in Cherwell in the army ordnance depot—well, something went wrong so me and one of the chief men in the office had a little falling out. So he said to me [angrily]:

"Where did you come from?"

'I said: "I come from that little place where the poet Crabbe described its sons as 'a wild amphibious race'."'

'He said: "Yes, you're a damned throwback!"'

'Speaking of Newson Garrett, there used to be man come down to Aldeburgh selling crockery; and he used to set it out in the road in a big square and he would stand in the middle and sell it by *Dutch auction*. Newson Garrett thought to himself in his *hoity* way:

"He don't want to be here!"

'He rode his horse right through the crockery and, of course, caused a bit of damage. Rode his horse all among the crockery, smashed it up. He was the *King of Aldeburgh*, and he thought he was going to do wonders; rode his horse through the crockery and broke up a lot of things. But there was a court job about it, and Newson had to pay. No, he wasn't popular with everybody; but, of course, it's like everything else, being an awkward old *hide*, he done a lot of good. Of course he did! 'cause he employed a lot of people in one way and another. He had these ships, you see, that used to take the malt from Snape up to London. So he employed a lot of people. My father went on his barges for a good many years.

'About my father's barge: there was one man did a little smuggling in Aldeburgh. When he brought his yacht up to the quay the coastguards went and searched it, and found he'd got more stuff than he should have—cigars and wine. So there were two coastguards left in charge of the boat. My father—his barge was going to be moved from the quay at Slaughden, in the night—so my father said to my brother and I:

"You boys, are you going to come and have a trip up the river in the barge?"

'So we went down; and the *coasties* could hear my father talking when we got back to his ship; and they called out:

"Come aboard! Come aboard!"

'So we went. My father took the boat and rowed us boys across to the yacht. So we went and spent an hour or so on the yacht. There was plenty of booze, plenty of wine. Quite a little evening. It interested us boys. That was about 1890. That would be eighty-three year ago.

'Of course when I was a boy there were five grocers' shops in Aldeburgh. Now there are only two: there were five bakers in

A Town Horseman

Aldeburgh, too. Mrs Ring: she had a baker's shop. She always used to say, tell folks:

"Keep your head up even if your behind is in the gutter!"

'But old Jack Spinks:

> *Jack Spinks is a baker of bread*
> *And ship's biscuits, so hard it is said.*
> *They would keep fresh for a year ;*
> *But there was always the fear*
> *They'd break half the teeth in your head!'*

5

In Service

———————————— ✳ ————————————

It has been said that the distinguishing mark of the upper-middle
and aristocratic classes used to be an easy poise, an assurance that
had its real base in the knowledge that there was always a good
dinner waiting for them and somebody at hand to cook and serve
it up. This may or may not be an exaggeration, but it is certainly
true that nothing has brought home to them the realities of the
gradual social revolution that has taken place during the past half-
century, more than the need occasionally to prepare their own
dinner and to stand in front of their own kitchen-sink doing the
washing-up. The domestic servant, now missing from most homes,
was for long one of the—often unwilling—props of the old social
order: the First World War changed that, or at least began a
change that has been accelerating ever since.

The entry of women into the armed forces during both wars,
into industry and onto the land, demonstrated that domestic service was not now the only outlet for a young girl. By the early
'thirties, as we gather from one of the following accounts, the
position of the domestic servant in London, for instance, had improved tremendously; not from any conscious effort to improve it
but simply because the Irish girl, the Welsh girl, or the girl from
the country, discovered that she need no longer stay in a place
where she was being exploited: servants had become scarce and
she could leave when she liked, certain of being able to find another
job without too much difficulty.

Miss Winifred Spence[1] (born 1891) was, in a real sense, well
trained for domestic service even before she entered it. She was
also inured to hard work and long hours, as one of the older members of a very large family; and she never questioned this dispen-
sation, accepting it as the lot she was born to. She knew no other
life; and, as it turned out, only the most demanding of employers

[1] *The Days That We Have Seen,* pp. 123–8.

could make conditions so harsh for her that she was compelled to leave. Her description of the prelude to her first job shows how well she had been trained in the admirable, smooth-running household of her parents:

'When I went to Oulton Broad, the lady that come for me to go —we knew her very well; in fact, she was godmother to one of my sisters—she wanted a cook. And I was away looking after my grandfather for a week or two, at the time; and that was in Blundeston. So my mother said she didn't think I'd be old enough to take a cook's place; but if she would like to come and see me she could. And the funny thing was—we always done our baking on a Friday, and I'd got a whole tableful of sausage rolls, things like you make for the week—and she asked me if I'd go and be her cook. And I told her I was afraid I wasn't old enough to take on anything like that. So she spotted what I'd made and she said:

"Well, who made those things?"

"I did."

"Well," she said, "if you can do that, what you don't know you could soon learn."

'So I went. But I was there only for a year and a half, because they went to Switzerland. I could have gone there with them; but my mother didn't want me to go; and I had a sister living there with me as parlourmaid. I was cook general, I suppose they call themselves now. My employers were independent people. While I was with them I started my day at 6 o'clock in the morning. I was very nervous when I first went; but I soon got used to it. There was a very nice housemaid when I first went. But she married and my sister took her place. I got on very well and I liked being there.

'I had the kitchen stove which was nothing but steel: I had to have to do that down every morning till you could see yourself in it; and whiten the hearth. I polished the steel with bath-brick; and I also had to do the morning-room stove. And that was all copper, and I had to clean that every morning with a kind of paste; and to do all the stairs and landings, and the rooms downstairs. And then, at half past eight, we used to have to get everything ready for breakfast and have it all ready; and then we had to go in for prayers. Then I cooked the breakfast. The master read the prayers (there were only two of us with the family now); and I well remember one incident. The housemaid said to me that the daughter and son-in-law were coming down for Easter (I've often had a laugh over this); and she said:

"Oh, he's a good-looking man! He *really is* a good-looking man!"

'Well, when we went in to prayers, I burst out laughing: I never saw anyone so ugly. And of course I had to go on the carpet about that, for laughing. Yes, and they asked me what I was laughing at; and of course I couldn't say their son-in-law was so ugly, so I said:

"Well, the housemaid said something to me before I came into prayers, and that just tickled me and I couldn't help it."

'So I got away with that all right.

'After we came out of prayers we had our breakfast, and went upstairs to make the beds and do the bedrooms. I used to help the housemaid to do that. I used to get on with the washing-up, see about the dinner and all the rest of the things. Monday morning was the laundry morning. On Monday we done all the washing. Nothing went to the laundry; and we had no one to help us—just me and the housemaid. We dried it outside; we had a nice little laundry-place. You could dry it in there in wet weather. The housemaid did any repairs, the needlework that wanted doing: that was the housemaid's job.

'We could have a rest in the afternoons, if we had time. Sometimes we had; sometimes we hadn't. We had an afternoon and evening once a week; and I had to be in at nine, not a minute later. And every other Sunday, afternoon and evening off; and the next Sunday, the morning to go to church. And we had our money once a quarter: half a crown a week. Then I had to save up and buy myself a black dress for the afternoons when the housemaid was out, you see. It took me quite a long time. We had to supply our own clothes: caps and aprons. Oh yes! caps and aprons. Oh yes! and stiff collars. I can't think what we looked like then! They always had dinner at night, about 7. They kept a lot of company. They always had somebody staying there; and we used to get into bed about 10 o'clock—later than that sometimes when they had a dinner party! Still, I was happy there.

'I had two places after that in which I didn't stop. One I stopped for five weeks; another I stopped for a year and a half. They had seven housemaids while I was there; and I got fed up with that place, so I left. The lady was the trouble, a bad-tem-

pered thing, too awkward. She couldn't keep anybody. She never
kept anybody more than three months. And when I stopped a
year and a half, they said I had broke the record! But I couldn't
stick it any longer. And I went from there to Elaine's—Mrs
Strutt's—aunt. I was with her till she died—for forty-two years.
So I kept the next place! That was at Oulton Broad too. We had
nine years living on the Broad—Mrs Briggs and I did—living on
a boat. That was lovely: I enjoyed that. We managed well. I did
all the errands (you know they don't deliver things), all weathers.
Oh, I loved it! There wasn't much housework to do; and it was
very warm, very cosy. The boat was about twenty-four feet long,
a houseboat called *The Swan*. We had a wireless set, one of the
first ones out, a crystal set; and of course a gramophone. We were
moored in a private dyke, and we used to have the gramophone on
deck. Yes, we were there till the war; and then Mrs Briggs's
sister didn't like her being there; and we went to Horning, to a
garden-house that belonged to them. And then she got a cottage
at Saxlingham. And she was there till she died. We were there
thirteen years. I still go to the Club [Old People's] at Saxlingham.'

Mrs Annie Cable (born 1893), of Kelsale in Suffolk,[1] relates her
experiences in service of a different kind. Instead of being a
domestic help to a private family she served as a member of a huge
domestic staff in large houses in Suffolk and Oxfordshire:

'I went to school in Kelsale and I left when I was fourteen.
After leaving I went into service at the Cupola, Leiston, as a
kitchen-maid. But it was very hard work: we had big old brass-
and copper-urns all the way round the kitchen. I used to have to
clean them with silver-sand, vinegar and salt. The Cupola—there
was a gentleman there who was a brother of Lord Huntingfield of
Huntingfield Hall, Heveningham. I expect you've heard of that.
As I was such a little thing, only just five foot high—and slim, it
was rather hard work; so my mother made me leave; got me this
place as a second still-room maid (I was always keen on cooking)
at Rendlesham Hall. I went there—I'd be sixteen when I went
there as second still-room maid; and I was there for just over two
years. And his lordship died; and the new lord, after paying death
duties, was unable to have such a big staff. Because there were

[1] *The Days That We Have Seen,* pp. 131-2.

seven housemaids, a chef, two kitchen-maids, and scullery-maid in the kitchen, and us two still-room maids in the still-room. We made all the cakes and biscuits, and the bottled fruit and jam—what I loved doing because it was most interesting work. No meat or anything like that; that we didn't have to do in the still-room. I liked it very much. I was there when his lordship died; and there was only one thing I was frightfully disappointed in: they allowed us £5 to buy some mourning for him. We all had to go into mourning. And, of course, we had to have a black dress for the afternoon, and black and white print dresses for the morning. £5 in those days meant a lot to a young girl of sixteen. I was so disappointed because the housekeeper made us go to a dressmaker. We had to have this black dress and the print dresses made. 'Course, I was hoping I was going to have a smart little costume, or something like a smart dress. We all had to pay for the lot: we all had to pay for the making of them; and all our £5 went!

'And as I told you the other day, we were allowed two-and-six a week beer-money, and two-and-six washing-money; and that was without our wages. We were paid once a month: our wages were £1 a month. Of course, that wasn't a lot; but with the beer-money and the washing-money we sort of like made a bit. We were on board-wages[1] three months in the year; and being in the still-room us two girls were a little bit crafty; and we saved sugar and tea and butter and flour; so we really had a good start when we came to keeping our two selves.

'We had to work very hard; up at 6 o'clock in the morning; and we were on the go till 10 o'clock at night. We were not allowed out after 5 o'clock: we had all to be in after the bell went at 5 o'clock. We were not allowed a bike; and of course we were not allowed to have anything to do with the men staff. There was a large men's staff there: a butler, Mr Webb, and seven gardeners in the bothy. And us still-room girls had to have to make them—we didn't have to put a cross on the buns—but we made the yeast buns every morning for their lunch; and one of them used to come in every morning for a tray full of buns. Poor old Mr Bootle drove the carriage, but just as I got there they got the motor-

[1] Wages given to servants in lieu of food, when the family was away from home and they were in charge of the house: *cf. Pretty Polly Perkins*:
She lived on board-wages, the house to keep clean,
For a gentleman's family in Paddington Green.

7 A shop in Camden Town (*c.* 1930): Robert Spindler

8 A Norwich *snob* (*c.* 1912) Mr Rix, Pottergate

cars and he was pensioned off. I was there for just over two years. I was very sorry to have to leave, because it was a marvellous house, you know. Previously, they'd had a fire there; and all the top rooms had never been properly finished: they were all just the bare walls and things round.

'There used to be—how many of us in the servants' hall? Us two, the still-room maids (we had breakfast in the still-room but for the rest of the meals we went into the servants' hall), the butler, his valet, the under-butler, the two footmen, the hall-boy, and the poor owd gentleman we called Daddy Ling. Daddy Ling must have been there when I was there: he used to be the stoker, down the stoke-hole with the big *hods*.[1] There was no *fridge* or anything like that there. But we had lovely cellars to keep all our stuff cool. No, we didn't have an ice-house. But they used to have ice from Woodbridge. There were some people by the name of Knights used to be carriers; and they used to come with like a pantechnicon —do you call it?—three times a week. They used to do our shopping in Woodbridge. And if us girls wanted anything like cottons or buttons or anything, and we used to have to give them three-pence extra for doing our shopping for us. They took for the staff there, and of course a lot of stuff for the house they used to get.

'If you had a boy? Oh, my word! Don't talk about that! That had to be on the *q.t.* There used to be Campsey Ash sports there— that's the next place to Rendlesham Hall, as you know; and they were on a Whit Monday; Framigan [Framlingham] Gala, Whit Tuesday. Well, one of the housemaids and myself, we got round the footman to let us out to go down to the sports. He said:

"Now when you come back be sure to tap on our window, and I'll come and let you in—provided the coast is clear."

'Because our housekeeper was a Miss Baker. And was she strict! She was elderly, and she'd been there for years with his lordship. Well, we got back there, and we kept tapping; but he didn't come. The housekeeper would have seen us. And if she had seen us, of course, we'd have been on the carpet.'

Mrs Cable is a ready and discursive speaker, and the phrase *on the carpet* reminded her of another occasion to which she imme-diately digressed. One often meets an informant like this, and the collector has to make up his mind whether to keep the speaker to

---

[1] Hod = a wooden vessel with a handle for holding coals—also a mortar board. Edward Moor, *Suffolk Words*, 1823.

her main theme by the prompting question or to allow her to
carry on in her own rhythm. My preference is to give the speaker
full rein: this, as in the present instance, usually proves itself to
be justified. After a long digression Mrs Cable eventually comes
back to the point where she is left outside the window with her
friend the housemaid and rounds off the incident. But if she had
been stopped in her flow we should probably not have had the
following, revealing 'carpet' episode that had been sparked off
merely by the phrase itself. It is better to make sure of getting the
full account even if it is told at disjointed length rather than to
risk interfering with a speaker's own mode of narration. Dis-
jointedness can always be remedied by editing the transcript;
or, if the story or incident needs to be heard as one continuous
narrative, by editing a copy of the tape or the tape itself. In my
view the collector of oral evidence should never attempt to dominate the interview but to guide it with the minimum interference
of the speaker's natural flow. Mrs Cable continues:

'I did go on the carpet once when I was there. I said to the head
still-room maid, this day:

"Will you let me make the cake for the drawing-room?" I had
been making the rolls and easy things, and rusks—we used to
make Suffolk rusks quite a lot. She said:

"Yes, I'll tell you how to do it."

'Well, when it went up into the drawing-room, unfortunately
for me they cut it; and there was a hole in it! So I had to march
up on to the carpet:

"Please! if you don't know how to make a cake you should not
be allowed to make any more until you know how to make it
properly!"

'So you can tell what it was like in them days.

'And as I told you, we had to wear little black caps on our
heads, nothing showy to church, not even in the summer-time.
We had to go very plain. We all had to walk into the pews[1] in
Rendlesham church and then shut the door. You've been in
Rendlesham church and may know that I'm telling the truth. And
the kitchen staff were not forced to go to church, but all us others
were. I used to go every other Sunday because one still-room maid
had to be left behind to do the toast and different things we had
to do: water-biscuits we had to make every morning. I had to do

---

[1] Box pews. See *Where Beards Wag All*, pp. 193–200.

them: we used to take it in turns. Well, one Sunday morning, the scullery-maid, a Scotch girl (a friend of mine; we corresponded for several years after we left) she said:

"Oh, I would so love to come to church!" I said:

"All right. Come with me then."

'Well, when we were coming back his lordship was in the front, and he happened to see us; and he came tearing down the steps to us and he says:

"Where is her bonnet?"

'Because she wasn't forced to go to church she hadn't got the bonnet. She'd not got one. So we explained:

"Well," he says, "if you are going to church, the next time you get yourself a bonnet. You can't go like that."

'So that will let you know—well, I don't know what they'd think of that today. Do you?

'But we managed over this affair [the incident she had digressed from]. And it was so funny, the housemaid—we were going on the roundabouts; and we'd each bought a little cane; and her cane got stuck into a young man's shoe as she was coming off the roundabout. And do you know? She got courting him, and she married him. Funny thing, she came to my wedding. She married a Mr Squirrel from Saxmundham. Wasn't it strange? She was second house-maid: Alice Threadgold her name was; and she was a Bungay girl, Earsham really (that's near Bungay). Her father was ill when I went to see him once. But he used to keep a public house there. And she married this Edwin Squirrel. We've often laughed about it—on those steam-horses, and the second footman letting us in!

'It was a tiring job. I've gone to bed many and many a time—and I was only sixteen—I've gone to bed many a time and laid on the bed and fell off to sleep before I was undressed because we were on the go the whole time. We used to have to get up at six and scrub out the still-room every morning. Very very particular they were. A beautiful house! Mind you, there was a lot of us, but still we did have to work long hours. And, of course, when we had a shooting-party, it was more like midnight before we went to bed. And I used to get round the head-one of the gardeners. He used to come in and do the flowers, all in the dining-room before the dinner was served; and it used to look glorious. Then quietly the butler would give us the down; and we used to slip in the stairs and look over the banisters and see all the ladies going into the dining-room—which was a great thrill. The still-room people and the kitchen-people never came in contact with the gentry, you see.'

Rendlesham Hall, rebuilt in 1871, was demolished just after the last war. In the reign of Edward VI the property was vested in the Spencer family. It passed to the fifth Duke of Hamilton who sold it to Sir George Wombwell. It was bought from him by Peter Isaac Thellusson, son of Isaac Thellusson who was ambassador for Geneva to the court of Louis XV. He later settled in London as a merchant; and in 1806 was raised as Baron Rendlesham to the Irish peerage. The Thellusson family was still at Rendlesham Hall after the First World War.

'He [Lord Rendlesham] used to have his own coffee—I suppose you would call them plantations, would you? But we used to have the beans come over green from France. We had to roast all them and then grind all our own coffee. And it used to be a most gorgeous smell. You can imagine when we used to go to Ipswich, to Limmers' there. They used to do it. And often I would think of Rendlesham Hall. He must have been a monied gentleman because it was a marvellous house. We had an excellent living. In the summer-time we used to have the whole rib of beef, cold with salad every Sunday; our joint was that. And all of us had to assemble in the servants' hall for lunch. In the winter we used to have it hot with Yorkshire pudding. Many a time I said to my husband:

"What would I give now to have a joint of beef like I had in those days!"

'Lord Rendlesham he used to distribute beef at Christmas-time in the villages. He did. And another thing—but not while I was there: Lady Rendlesham died before I went there—but this daughter, Miss Celia Thellusson, another thing she used to do was to have what they called a baby's basket; and she went round the village. Anyone who was very poor, she used to lend them this baby's basket, full of all the baby's linen, and blankets. And then she would come into us and have us make some cakes and different things; and she would take them to them. They were very good to the people in the village. They were very very strict over who they gave to. If they thought it was anyone who hadn't behaved themselves, they got no sympathy from the Rendlesham family. They were very very old Victorian people, you know. So was Miss Thellusson, really. Though I only saw her once to speak to, Miss Thellusson. Through the cake getting a hole in it!

'I can always remember once, the head footman coming in once for the tea-tray. Us still-room people done all the tea. The kitchen people done breakfast, lunch and dinner at night. We always done all the tea, the cakes and everything. Well, this afternoon the tall housemaids were then going by to have their tea (they had their own sitting-room, the housemaids did); they came down the stairs. So I happened to say to the footman, I say:

"Why can't I be like some of them girls!"

'He say: "Look . . ."

"Some of them are nearly six foot," I said, "And here I am, very small, very short," and I was very slim in those days.

'He said:

"My dear! You don't want to worry," he says. "All men admire the big ones, but they *love* the little ones!"

'So I said: "That's a little bit o' comfort I get then for being small!"

'We were allowed a dance once a week, because—as I told you—we were not allowed out after five; but we were allowed a dance. The valet used to play the violin for us; and they told me I should learn to dance. I should learn if I had a light chair and danced round with that chair; and they told me the steps. My word! I couldn't get on with that! so I'm afraid I wasn't a very good dancer.—If we'd ha' been caught the night the footman let us in at 10 o'clock that would have been the sack for us. We'd have been instantly dismissed! The housekeeper, Miss Baker, after his lordship died—she was very nice, very firm, very strict. And when I first went there, I had to do out their sitting-room which was on the ground floor, the same as our still-room. (The valet, the head footman and the butler and the housekeeper shared that sitting-room in the afternoon, for their tea. I didn't have to take their tea in, because the under-footman used to have to take that in.) And Miss Baker came in to show me how to turn out a room. So I said:

"Well! I've been in service before."

'She said: "Never mind! You must do it my way," she says. "Now look. You don't want to worry about the middle. The middles will take care of theirself. Never forget to go in the corners!"

'Because it was a most beautifully furnished place, naturally. And when you had to turn out, you'd got to move everything:

"Now don't forget," she said, "when you turn out a room, don't worry about the middle of the room, the corners are the most important."

'So *that* I always thought about.

'I was there at Rendlesham Hall just over two years; and then I went to Viscount Harcourt at Newnham Park, Oxfordshire. Oh! that really was a most marvellous place. I used to help make their household bread: two hundred loaves at the time, three times a week. We made all our own bread. There was a tremendous big staff there. There was the nursery, the school-room, and the drawing-room: there were three lots. And they used to come and give us the pattern, what the butler got to lay on the table; the tea-service would be the same pattern as the table-cloth was. Of course, we had—King Edward VII came down there. I was still under-housemaid, because you had to be very clever to be a head housemaid or head still-room maid; and I said:

"You'll let me make the cakes?" (I was getting quite good then, although I say it myself) and I said: "Now the King is here. So I really can say I've been *Cake-Maker to the King!*"

He came down; Lloyd George came down—they were all Liberal people. Lord Rendlesham was strict Conservative; but they were Liberals, the Harcourts were at Newnham Park. Lloyd George came there; Mr Asquith come there. Then I was not very well: I had a bad back. I don't know whether it was being too close to the river there. I come home; met my husband; and we got married. Sixty-nine year ago this September [to her husband]. Think of it, dear! We should have been married in August; but he was in camp with the Territorials and war broke out. We got married when he had a forty-eight-hours leave in September [1914].

'Yes, I made a cake for Edward VII. Whether he eat any of it I don't know! But listen! The footman there had to powder their faces, they did, really! And wear gloves. Gloves! And they used to bring us girls chocolates; because when they were coming out of the dining-room, anything nice (they hadn't time to take off their gloves) anything nice that was left in the dishes they used to pinch a piece and eat it. And the finger and thumb had always got stained, you see. So us girls used to wash their gloves out for them; and they used to buy us chocolates. In the still-room we had plenty of hot water.

'They had five girls there to do the laundry-work; done all their own laundry at Newnham Park. It was a lovely place. And I always remember going through the gates there. It was raining hard; and when you went through the gates (they were very strict again there: just the same!) and we used to have to call out to the lodge-keeper, and they used to have a lever in the lodge to open the gate. So she said to us two girls one day:

"Now what are you going out for on a rainy day? What are you going to do?"

"Oh," we said, "we thought we'd like a walk, and we want to go to the post."

'She say: "I can quite believe that!" she say. "You know they say: *Love will draw where a donkey won't.*" '

Mrs Sturgeon, another native of Suffolk, told me how she went into service, first in Suffolk and later in London. She was born in 1917, and therefore describes a period later than Miss Spence and Mrs Cable. Mrs Sturgeon was Happy Powley before she married, daughter of a well-known East Anglian wherry-man, Jack Powley, skipper of the *Albion*.[1] Her unusual Christian name is an old family name, and not—as she says—a piece of modern fancy:

'I went to service in a small country town, at fourteen—straight after I left school. It was a big house. There was myself and another girl: we ran the whole house; and they were waited on at table; two of us waited on them; two of us laid out. They thought they'd got a valet and staff. Oh, that was dreadful! We worked from morning till night, morning till night. And I went there as a privilege, for doing most well at school! I got the prize for domestic science and for being the best pupil. So I was allowed to go there and work for one of the big men of the town. There was a big scullery, and I did all the cooking on a big old—a huge stove in the kitchen; and there were great big iron pots you could hardly lift. They used to have dinner parties, and the doctors used to come, and all the posh people; and we had to do all the cooking

[1] *Black Traders*, Roy Clark, London, 1961, pp. 66, opp. 144, 154.

and all the waiting on the table. I had five shillings a week, and Alma—the girl that was with me—had five and six because she was six months older than me.

'There was only two of them in the family; but they used to have tennis parties. The *Imps* [Junior Imperial League], the young Conservatives, they used to come to tea after the tennis parties; and we had to go and wait on them, and see to them. And oh! you could have a chapter about Saturday afternoon when we had to do the flues, and do the kitchen out, scrub the back yard and chop all the sticks. The Master used to go shooting, and he once brought a rabbit in and threw it into the kitchen. We had to prepare that; but I had no idea how to skin a rabbit; I'd never seen my mother do it. But you were supposed to do it. I took it outside where there was a place you chopped wood in, at the back. We took this rabbit outside to the chopping block. And I daren't look as I brought down the chopper: I chopped its head off across the shoulders. We got the skin off somehow; and we had to cook this rabbit, and make it into a rabbit stew. And I didn't know about cleaning out the back passage: I thought it was clean because it had been *hulked*.[1] And, of course, that was the piece the Master got on his plate. There was such a roar from the dining-room. But he still ate it! He shouted about it but he still ate it! We could laugh about it afterwards; but we couldn't laugh about it at the time; we were too frightened.

'Another incident we've laughed about since. We used to be allowed out on alternate Sundays in the afternoon. The other girl had the morning off because she sometimes went to the Church of England; but me being Congregational, that didn't count as Christianity: I didn't get any time off for going. Anyway, one Sunday morning we had boiled a *spotted-dog*, a suet pudding in a cloth, a long sausage-shaped one. And there was—I know! the drains had blocked that morning; and you daren't tell them the drains had blocked because they always say: "That's something you've put in it!" So we got some long rods out in the back yard, and we'd taken the grating off and we were pushing these rods through. But we daren't stop long enough because we got to dish the dinner up. So we took the pudding outside to empty the water out of the saucepan, so we got the pudding out. Well, of course, the grating was still off the drains and the pudding went down!

[1] Disembowelled.

In Service

And we were poking about trying to get this pudding out; and we had to lift the *flags* [flag-stones] up. It wasn't a pipe; something like a half-pipe; and when we got the flags up we retrieved the pudding! Then we poured some boiling water over it and served it up! Our life was full of episodes like this because you never could say you'd done anything wrong because you'd be sure to *get it*.

'Oh, it was terrible! I had the kindest mother; but, you see, she said:

"This is what it is to work for your living! All the others had to do it. This is just what you have to do." We used to have Wednesday afternoon off from about half past three to nine. You could never go to the pictures [films] because you had to come out in the middle of the picture. You couldn't do anything or go anywhere. You came in at 9 o'clock because it wasn't fit for young girls to be out. It wasn't right! They didn't know what you'd been up to. So we just used to go home for that time and have a rest. And then there were the clothes you had on in the morning: your morning-dress and your morning-cap to cover your head all up, your apron. And I had to clean the step—you look at that step when you next go past there. It's marble, and it was the most *wonderful* doorstep! And I used to have to scrub that every morning; and I used to be scrubbing that when all the boys I'd been to school with were going up to the works. And, do you know, you had old black stockings on; and, of course, you're growing quickly at that age—the dresses, you'd soon grown out of them. And they were ever so short; and there was I scrubbing the step trying to keep the dress down and not to show my leg. Oh, the agony!

'The other one, Alma, she had to do the door. It was a *marvellous* door. Oh, my word! It was oak; and she had to clean it; clean the brass, and into the little creases. But no Brasso must go on the oak of the door. Everything had to be—I wasn't allowed to scrub that step in the ordinary way because you'd mark the marble. It had really to be washed down and you had to make a solution of starch and put over it; and even where it curved under you had to get all the dirt out of there as well. This was before breakfast. And there was lighting that great stove so that the water had to be hot enough for the Master to shave with. But you mustn't roar it up because the Master paid so-and-so for the coal. You must

73

never roar it to make it hot! Oh, I know! I had to do the study before breakfast. Well, no Hoover: it was carpet; you had to sweep the carpet. And he had all alongside—whips, right from long carriage whips right down to little riding crops. And they stood on the lino between the carpet and the wall. You had to dust round them. And if you touched one, the lot went down! But you still got to dust behind them; and if you stood them up after they'd fallen, and there was one out of place, there was some shouting!

'You were worried all the time: you couldn't do things properly. And on his desk he had horses and hounds, all carved in wood. And you had to have all that polished before breakfast and all the hounds in exactly the same place. You were scrabbling, hurrying over everything: and yet everything had to be perfect. You had to get the breakfast then: bread and milk for the Master. You had to cut his bread for his bread and milk in squares; and it mustn't be crumbly, and all the squares had to be the same size. And then, they didn't have breakfast like ordinary people have, they had kedgeree. It took a bit of making: you had to cook the rice and potatoes and fish and a hard-boiled egg chopped up in it. And cups of tea and then toast. With the toast, you had to hold it on a fork in front of the fire; you couldn't do anything else while you were holding this toast. Alma had just as many things to do before breakfast. Oh my word! and that went on all day, evening as well, because they had dinner in the evening.

'I had to cook the dinner, and Alma had just as much to do. Although there was only two of us there we rarely saw each other. We didn't have time to talk because she was about the pantry seeing to all the silver and the glass and that; and I was out in the back scullery and the kitchen. So I cooked the dinner and she laid the table—very elaborate, you see; not allowed to touch the silver with her hands. When she laid the table she wasn't allowed to touch a fork with her fingers. All had to be done with chamois leather. And ooh! such a roaring and such a telling-off if there was a thumb-mark on the silver. But I didn't have to do that. That was Alma's job. And she'd take the first—you know, they always had silver entrée dishes—she'd take the first round, serving as if you'd got a staff of a hundred; lay them on the table properly; and I had to walk behind her. I'd changed from my cooking-set I was wearing into my parlourmaid set with the frilly cap. Then I had to go behind her with the vegetables. All the time I was worrying what was going on in the kitchen. I don't know how I did it! I couldn't do it now.

'All sauce-bottles were kept in the sideboard; and they all had a mark on them with the date in pencil so that—in case you took any. The wine? We never saw the wine: that was locked up and only came out at a dinner party. We were always tired; always unhappy; we really were, because you could never keep up with the work. For instance, if they went out to dinner, you didn't get an evening free; you had to polish the brass or something—they had enormous brass-pieces—or some task would be given to make sure you were kept going until bed-time.

'And another time—Madam, the mistress, used to come out into the kitchen every morning and weigh out the flour and fat that you needed for cooking during the day. And one day for lunch they had a kind of *loaf*, with a tin of salmon and mashed potatoes—something again that went a long way and what was cheap. They always had three or four courses; but they were always things like that. There was some of it over, and she sent it out on a side-plate, all forked up nicely. I put it in the *safe* (we didn't have a *fridge* then). Now we were always hungry, always hungry: you know when you're growing. When this dish came out, I got the fork and had a mouthful and forked it up again; put it back in the safe for the next morning. 10 o'clock she came into the kitchen: she always used to look at things that were left over and what could be cooked and made up. And she came out holding this piece of salmon loaf, and called me; and she looked at me. She said:

"Have you eaten any of this?"

"No, Ma'am." I was terrified.

"Oh, a liar as well as a thief!"

'You see, now with our upbringing they were the two worst things you could say to anybody. And you *were* a liar and a thief: she was right! The attitude all the time, you see, was that they were tolerating you. You really believed you were like that!

'But you see, not to grumble! because she [the Mistress] was doing us a favour. She was training us! You always had to have that feeling: how kind she was that she was showing us the right way to do it. And you had that feeling! How was it that you weren't appreciating what she was doing? You had to be brought up like that after all, because your parents knew that that's what you had to do. It would have been wrong of them to have brought you up differently, wouldn't it? Because, you know, you mustn't answer back or anything.

'We used to go up these back-stairs. We were terrified, you see, going up these back-stairs; that was so dark! We never set foot on the front-stairs. That was a terrible thing. That was a crime! to put your foot on the front-stairs. The Master paid so much for that carpet and you weren't allowed to wear it out. (It was always what the Master paid for.) Everything—well, we were being wasteful with their possessions and spoiling them. So we had to go up the back-stairs right to the top of the house, to these attics—one each—bare boards. Well, my room was at the top of the stairs. Alma had to go through three empty attics to get to her room; and, of course, she was frightened, and she'd stop in my room. She said: "Come into my room with me." Well, after I'd been there I'd be too frightened to come back. So we used to stop and sleep in this one bed because we were frightened, cold and miserable; and howling and crying half the time. So we were in this bed, Alma's bed; and Ma'am came upstairs:

"Oh!" she said, "the Master paid so much for that mattress. That's for one to sleep on! Why are you here?"

'Oh, I know what we'd got, what wicked thing we were doing! We'd got film-magazines in bed, looking at them with the candle on. Film-magazines! Well, she whoolly carried on as if we were doing something dreadful:

"Why are you both in the same room?"

"Well, Alma was frightened to come through those empty attics."

"Stupid things! Frightened! Who do you think is going to be out there?"

'You know, she really made us feel we were doing something dreadful. We were reading the film-magazines and we never saw the "pictures" they described! Well, we felt quite depraved after she'd finished with us.

'We had to do everything. For instance, they had gas-lighting; and we had to go and light the gas and have it very low, all over the house. So that when they went into the bedroom they just had to pull the little chain down and the light came on. You see, you were always worried about things: you mustn't light them before it got dark; on the other hand, if you waited till it was too dark you couldn't see to light them. Apart from that, there was these big empty rooms, and we were frightened. And you always had to draw the curtains; but you were always told off if you'd drawn them too soon, or if you hadn't drawn them. So you had always to be thinking about the right time to do these things. The beds used to be turned down, lay the night-dresses and pyjamas out. You know, they were waited on as if they had a large staff. We went at it all day like that. I can honestly say, I never remember, never remember sitting down to eat anything; because there was so much work piling up behind you, you had got to get on with; and because you couldn't be sitting down in case somebody come in.

'Saturday afternoon was a very *enjoyable* time: this was *The Day of the Flues*. After lunch you had to do the flues. The flues in the kitchen-range! You made a lot of mess, all the soot flying about. But you got as much soot out of the stove as you could. Of course, I knew I couldn't do it properly because there were so many crannies; you couldn't get all the soot out; all little trap-doors you had to undo, under the oven and over the oven and all that. Then there was a big wooden dresser all along the side of the kitchen; everything had to come off that and be washed; and it had to be scrubbed down; scrub the tables, scrub the chairs, clean the stove—clean it, polish it with blacklead; and after it had been polished it was supposed to be shining. Then do the floor. The floor was of red tiles; and you were only allowed to do so much of the floor with the same water, you know, so that the water mustn't be dirty. Of course, the water wasn't hot in the stove so you had to heat the water up on one of these saucepans. How I lifted them I don't know! Then we had to do the back scullery. Scrub the back yard on your hands and knees. And then it was time to start on the Saturday evening's dinner.

'Well, when you'd just finished with the floor—sometimes, but not often, my word! I think I'd have gone mad!—you'd hear Ma'am come stamping down the corridor. She come into the kitchen; she'd have rubber gloves, a long *mac* and her hair tied up:

"Have you done the flues properly?"

"Yes, Ma'am."

'Right! Then she'd go and do those flues again. Of course,

every time you do that you can get soot, can't you? And there'd be soot over everything: the whole lot to do again. And she got out a brush and did the oven door. Now the oven door is the least greasy part of the stove; and she got the brush and she'd go and polish vigorously, as hard as she could:

"I want it to look like that all over."

'I used to say it never would have worried me if I'd joined a concentration camp!

'I stayed at this job one year. It was through the flues how I came to . . . I lost that good job! That was a shame! My sister Mary, my elder sister, was getting married, so I was going to be bridesmaid. She came the Saturday before the wedding, and I was doing the flues. She was with my cousin from London, Ella, a very headstrong sort of girl. And they came round. What a cheek! They came to the back door! We were never allowed to have anybody come to the back door. And they come in, and I was in the middle of doing the flues. And Ella said:

"Whatever are you doing, gel? Has she fell out with the bloody sweep? You shouldn't be doing this!"

'And she was using some language, you know; and my sister Mary said:

"What you doing this on a Saturday afternoon for? Leave the blessed place! Come to London with me."

'Madam—she'd heard all this because she was always listening behind the green-baize door; and when they'd gone she came into the kitchen:

"I never want that class of person to come into my house again! You dare have such people in my house!"

'And I was frightened because it was my own sister and my cousin. Well, the following Saturday my sister got married. I had only two hours off for my sister's wedding. I was bridesmaid; and I had all that grime: my hands were always rough with being in hot soda-water: they were always dirty. You never felt clean. But I had a good bath; and there I had to go and be a bridesmaid, and get back within two hours. And there was all the lovely wedding reception I missed. Well, it was only in our house; but it seemed lovely to us. And I had to go back to work. But I mean: how would they manage without me!

'Later my sister said to me: "Oh, hang it all! You aren't going to stop there. You come up to London with me." And that's how

I went to London. My sister and her husband set up house in
Sydenham; and I went up and stayed with them till I got a job at
Forest Hill. That was an improvement. Well, it couldn't have
been worse.—I'd been in the Suffolk job for a year; and that
wasn't ancient times I've been telling you about. That was in 1932.
But the war altered that: it killed all that!'

Mrs Sturgeon's account of her service in a small country town
and her later experience in London illustrates one particular
aspect of the value of taking evidence from living people. In describing her work in a middle-class household she reveals the
social attitudes of a harsh, Victorian paternalism or authoritari-
anism, long surviving its demise or at least its modification, in the
cities and industrial areas. It shows by giving specific local and
detailed evidence that social change is far from being uniform (a
truism, perhaps, but one we need to have constantly before our
eyes). It illustrates that the effective diffusion of ideas and attitudes
throughout the country must not be taken for granted, in spite of
the growth of mass communication through the daily newspaper
from the start of this century. New ideas, new social attitudes do
not take real root until the soil—the material conditions—is ready
for them. There in Suffolk, in the 'twenties and early 'thirties, in
spite of the erosion of the old attitudes by the upheaval of the
First World War, there was little real change. Farming was in the
doldrums; no new industry of any sizeable scale had moved in;
unemployment was high, and there was hardly any alternative for
a young girl leaving school except domestic service. There was no
shortage of labour of this kind, therefore, and no need to adjust
old attitudes. You could still tell a girl she had to be indoors by
9 o'clock; you could still dress her up, thus reinforcing her consciousness of her proper station; you could still make her dance
through a fantastically out-dated table ritual without any real fear
of losing her services. Social attitudes, in other words, tend to
have an inertia that only real changes in social conditions will
effectively overcome. Mrs Sturgeon recognizes this herself when
she infers that not only were her employers socially conditioned
to expect unquestioning service on their own terms, but that she
and her parents had also been conditioned—if not altogether fully
—to concede that this service was their employers' right, or at

least the inescapable reality with which they had to contend. Although the contrast between her Suffolk and her later, London employers was extremely marked—and she comments on the humanity of these as much as the harshness of the others, thus inferring that it was due to individual attitudes or idiosyncrasies—she puts her finger on the real reason for the contrast in the first sentences of the following account of her London experience:

'In London I was fortunate. It was getting on to the end of that time really, and now servants were harder to get. You could leave, you see; you'd get somewhere else. And that was the only way: to leave your job and go somewhere else. Forest Hill—that was all right because it was an elderly lady and her husband and a grown-up daughter. They were very nice people, and I was the only one there. But the old couple died, and the daughter wanted me to be a companion. She was getting on, and at my age then—sixteen—I didn't feel I wanted to be a companion.

'Then I worked in the Tower of London—in the King's House; well, it's the Queen's House now—in the Tower where the Governor lived; and I worked for the Governor. It was quite interesting; well, very interesting. But they'd been in India, and she was a bit—had old ideas; she was used to dealing with natives. After that I worked for Charles Laughton, the actor, and his wife Elsa Lanchester, the actress. They lived in Gordon Square, and were on the fringe of the Bloomsbury set. There were two of us: Nellie, the cook, and me. We lived in a maisonette—the top three floors; and the bottom three floors were offices. All the servants in the Square knew one another; and Nellie, the cook that worked with me, knew Lottie—Clive Bell's cook; she was very friendly with her; and we used to go over there if they had any luncheons. Clive Bell, Mrs Bell—Vanessa Bell, Virginia Woolf, Lady Violet Bonham-Carter, no not Lytton Strachey, John Strachey, Leonard Woolf, and Maynard Keynes, he was often there. Lord . . . he was the most famous of the lot . . . why can't I remember his name: Lord Russell! Bertrand Russell. And, of course, that was something so different for me because they treated you like one of themselves. No cap, no apron or anything. No *Sir* or *Madam*; and this was marvellous! You did your work, and there you are! No waiting at table.

'We knew all these people, and they talked to you using your Christian name. And they would talk to you—you know, as if you

9 A nursemaid with her charge (*c.* 1890)

10 Man wearing a velvet jacket

11 Old couple

12 A coastguard (or customs?) officer and family

could read and write. And they had discussions with you. Now that was lovely, that was! I can remember Virginia Woolf at dinner parties and that. But Nellie who was with me, she'd been her cook: Nellie Boxall. She worked for her for eighteen years. But she had to leave because she was a bit highly strung; and of course you know Virginia herself was. Oh, she was lovely—she was always, sort of the grand lady. And her sister, too; we used to go round to theirs for parties. Clive Bell's wife, Vanessa, and Duncan Grant: they had a studio in Fitzroy Street. And when they had a party, Lottie, who was Clive Bell's cook—well, she did everything for him—she'd say:

"There's a party round Fitzroy Street!"

'So we used to go round. Heaven knows who we used to see at the Fitzroy Street parties: we didn't know half the people that were there: we only knew the family. That's at Mrs Bell's parties —Mr Bell didn't use to go. Mrs Bell and Duncan Grant, they shared a studio; they used to live together at Fitzroy Street. They used to have exhibitions of their pupils' work; and we went there to help Lottie and showed people in, and we'd put little *pinnies* on to start with. We'd dress up in our party things; just put a little *pinny* on to start; unpack the things from Fortnums, put them onto plates. And as soon as Mrs Bell went to bed—she used to retire quite early—there you are! We were at the party.

'As I say, the servants in the Square all knew each other. Now Lottie, she was a character. She was picked up on the doorstep. She was a gypsy: she looked a gypsy. And they sort of took her in. She posed for all these different artists. But she looked after Mr Bell and his wife and their children: Angelica, Quentin and Julian. Quentin was a potter. He used to make pots and Vanessa his mother used to paint them. I can remember they had a big display in Heal's of Tottenham Court Road of Quentin's pots. Julian was killed in Spain. One day Lottie came back—she used to go down to the country house when they all went down there together—coming back and saying:

"Oh, Julian went off. His mother was crying. And he just went off up the road. He's gone to Spain!"

'He got killed out there. He was a nice boy.

'The first time I ever saw Bertrand Russell he came in—this was a party at the Bells' house. And I was downstairs with Lottie; and we were taking coats, do you see; people were coming in to lunch or dinner—I forget—we were taking the coats, and a man went upstairs—I don't know who he was—and he had a big head, and it was completely bald! The next person to come in was Bertrand Russell. And Lottie slapped him on his back and said:

"Do you know what! There's a man just gone upstairs, and he's got a head like a bladder of lard!"

'Russell laughed, and we all laughed: she knew him as well as that. They would talk to you about things. You had an opinion. You *could* have an opinion about things. They would ask:

"What do you think about so-and-so?" and I would say:

"What does it matter what I think?"

"Of course it matters!" they'd say: "You've got an opinion like everyone else!"

'So I liked to stay in the room with Lottie at these parties: I wanted to listen to the conversation. On one occasion Lottie had made this casserole thing, and she'd got this herb-bag—*bouquet garni*—in it. After she'd finished serving it she said suddenly:

"I can't find the herb-bag! Can't find the herb-bag!"

'And she hunted in all their plates, fishing for the *bouquet*, fishing in everybody's plate for the herb-bag:

"Oh, Lady Violet! You've got the herb-bag?"

'And she fished it out of her plate! She was a character. They all knew her; everybody knew her. She used to go down to Knole to Vita Sackville West's, Harold Nicolson's wife. She was related someway round to the Bells. And Clough Williams-Ellis and his wife Amabel used to be in Knole and at these parties in Fitzroy Street. Of course, Maynard Keynes and Lydia Lopokova, the ballet dancer, they were often there. He used to be *The Professor* and she *Madam Keynes*—This is Lottie:

"He's A BIG MAN, you know: UP AT CAMBRIDGE, you know!"

'We never really knew how important they were when we were there with them. Maynard Keynes wasn't one of the most forthcoming of them, the most friendly. Bertrand Russell, particularly, would talk to you and ask you what you thought. He really minded what you told him. And all those years [before] when you weren't allowed to have an opinion!

'It was all so interesting: there was an old lady called Pepita. I think Lord Sackville-West, he went to Spain when he was very young, married her and brought her back. She was Vita Sackville-West's mother; she was an old lady then, a widow. And on one occasion Nellie and Lottie looked out of our back window and said:

"Do you remember when Pepita used to be over there? If the sellers of paper-flowers came round with, perhaps, a barrow full, she'd buy the lot! Then she'd stick them all in the garden. All the garden was full of paper-flowers. It didn't matter if it was winter-time or what, they'd be there till it rained on them."[1]

'Then we used to see Edith Sitwell go past with her cloak flying in the breeze. She used to live in the Square, I think; she must have lived in the Square, because she used to walk in the gardens, in the middle of the Square, with the railings round them. You could then.

'We used to see a lot of theatrical people at the Laughtons'. Elsa Lanchester, Charles Laughton's wife, acted with him in films. They were very nice to work for; and many interesting people would come. Somerset Maugham, when they did *The Vessel of Wrath*, he used to come for dinner. He'd always smell nice: he always had a button-hole. We went down two or three times to see *The Vessel of Wrath* being made at the studios. Eric Palmer was the director. Charles Laughton was very good in that film, the Somerset Maugham story. Mrs Laughton was the missionary's sister; and Mr Guthrie was the missionary. Do you know that story? Charles Laughton was the beachcomber. That was most interesting watching that being made. Mr Guthrie—Tyrone Guthrie—was a big tall man. He was *Sir* before he died: ever such a nice, kind man: he always wore carpet-slippers. Larry Adler, the harmonica player, used to come to the Laughtons' as much as anyone. Mrs—Benita Jaeger who married John Armstrong: she used to be Mr Bell's secretary. And she used to be—she lived in the flat with Mr Bell—anyway, she was his secretary, and used to go with him to Paris and all those places to look at pictures, to write about pictures. He was an art-critic wasn't he, Clive Bell? She used to be his secretary. Then she married John Armstrong who was an artist. Mrs Armstrong was there more than anybody. She was Mrs Laughton's very best friend, a very, very

[1] The story about Pepita is not accurate as it stands. Pepita, the Spanish dancer (died 1871), was the grandmother of Vita Sackville West. Nellie and Lottie were probably confusing her with her daughter Victoria, Vita's mother (born 1862, in Paris).

beautiful woman; very, very beautiful and intelligent—extremely beautiful woman.

'But they were all so nice and friendly; and everybody who came to the house was friendly, and they called you Happy. The Bloomsbury set, they treated us well. Oh, yes! Because when you're in service [as I was in Suffolk] you'd think:

"What . . . why am I doing this? Why should I do this? And those young people who are still at school and haven't got any of this to do, just being waited on! Why, why, why?"

'And you'd think, it's me who's peculiar for asking why. Why not? That's how things were at the time. Then, when you get in with people like those at the Laughtons', you knew there were other people who thought like you did.

'That was the contrast between my experience in London and in Suffolk with those people what my mother used to call *Half-sixes*![1] people who thought they were! The sherry set! The people in Gordon Square they were all *doing* something, weren't they? Their attitude was: "We get paid a lot of money for doing what we do: you don't get paid as much for what you do. But that's just how it is. It doesn't mean that we are better than you." That meant you still had your dignity. They never put you down. For instance, at the Laughtons', when they had friends in to dinner, you didn't wait at the table; they never had all this elaborate waiting on like they had in the job I had in Suffolk; you didn't have any of that nonsense. You took the food in and put it on the table; and they'd even bring their plates out. They'd clear the table themselves and put the dirty things on the side; and help to take the other things in. I've seen Marlene Dietrich carry out dirty plates, because she used to come quite often. Standing outside on the landing there was a cupboard; and they'd bring the things out there; and if they wanted something, they'd shout: HAPP-AY! There were no caps and overalls and things like that; just an overall to keep your dress clean.

'Well, it all broke up when the War came—1939. Mr and Mrs Laughton went to America just before the War began; and I went home. And I joined the Army as a cook the day after the War broke out. Then during the War I got married.'

There is little need of any observations on the above. Mrs Sturgeon speaks effectively for herself and for those who were in

[1] Presumably, people who had reached only half the score.

service. But it is worth pointing out that here there is also a view of a well-known and historically significant group of people, seen from an entirely fresh angle. After hearing her evidence one can hardly escape the conviction that although the Bloomsbury group has, for one reason or another, been much maligned both in and outside literary circles, they did at least treat their servants well —as human beings; and this, so it appears, was out of moral conviction and not out of any selfish policy.

6

Dress in Town and Country

———————————※———————————

After taking oral evidence for some time in the field, the student will no doubt become aware that the boundaries of conventional history are much too narrow and rigid. Dress and costume, for instance, rarely come under the local historian's scrutiny, yet a good argument can be made out for considering it as an essential part of social history. For apart from its obvious functions of protection from wind, sun and weather, and of adornment and display, dress has the less conscious function of being one form of social affirmation. By dressing yourself in a certain way, you are consciously or unconsciously aligning or identifying with a certain class or group in society; or, on the other hand, you may be making it known that you belong to no class or group and that you are 'travelling' on your own. For in spite of the increasing standardization of dress due to mass production, there is still great scope for individual *statement* where unmistakable signals can be sent simply by the wearing of certain articles of apparel, or by the total costume itself.

Before the First World War, however, dress was more rigidly limited both by the class and the occupation of the wearer: it was the mark of a more stratified and more authoritarian society. Although there were no explicit sumptuary rules—with obvious exceptions, like the armed services, the post office, the police, the railways, the big houses and so on—the general expectation was that a man should dress according to his station. Each tradesman had his particular dress, and he was usually proud of it. I remember recording a retired blacksmith about fifteen years ago: he worked in a small country town and he told me how he had noticed the change in dress during his working life. In his younger days he would walk into the street in his leather apron, go to the pub or the post office still wearing it: he was proud of it. All the craftsmen and tradesmen felt the same. The butcher wore his distinctive apron in the street and perhaps a straw hat to go with it. The grocer whose long, fringed apron reached down right to his ankles, tucked one corner of his apron into the tape around his waist, as he came from behind his counter, to give his legs greater ease of movement as he went outside. The diagonal line of the apron now revealed one trouser leg. In addition to making his walking easier it was also a signal that he was not ashamed to be identified; and although he was for the moment off duty he was still ready at the appearance of a customer to slip back behind the counter and let down his apron.

The late Harry Sexton of Sexton Sons and Everard, the Norwich shoe manufacturers, once lectured on the shoe industry in Norwich between about 1870 and 1914. He confirmed that the workmen in the industry, the *snobs*, were to be seen in the streets in their white aprons: they wore them even when they were not working. He had collected, out of his own experience, a great amount of information about the industry, and he gave a clear picture of how it was organized at the beginning of the century. There were relatively few factories, and two-thirds of the work was done in the home. Attached to each factory were *garret masters* who employed their own men to make the upper part of the shoes either in their own homes (in garrets) or in specially built sheds. The only operations done in the factory were *clicking*[1] and sole-cutting. The home workers were a common sight in the Norwich streets as they carried their shoes on poles to hand in at the *wicket* of the factory. Their white aprons, and their appearance generally, got more and more bedraggled as the week went on. The women carried their work, chiefly machining, to the factory in old perambulators.

On the farm, too, there was a tremendous pride in occupational dress.[2] Most trades and professions had a prescribed if unofficial 'uniform'. In the professions this—if not always business-black— was dark and correct. It was easy to pick out the leisured classes; and being the most conservative they tended to stick longer to their old manner of dress when the changes began. The First World War was the watershed in dress as in much else. Dress

[1] The cutting out of the upper part of the shoe from the leather skin, a very skilled job.

[2] *The Horse in the Furrow,* Chapter 6; *The Farm and the Village,* Chapter 12.

changed as the old society broke up; and the subtlety and variety of the signals sent out in the interim period, when it was becoming difficult to tell a person's class merely by looking at his clothes, were fascinating. To give an example: in Cambridge during the 'thirties it was already becoming difficult to place a man's class by his appearance: the tweed jacket and the flannel or worsted trousers—successors to the Oxford *bags*, and often worn to the point of shabbiness—were the norm, especially among the younger men, irrespective of class or status. Nevertheless, if you found a stranger taking a surreptitious interest in your tie or your shoes, you knew immediately that he was finding out whether you belonged to the same class as he did—naturally the right class. For the quality of tie or shoes was supposed to be an infallible method of placing.

It is suggested that the local historian may well find it worthwhile to be interested in the contrast between the informality of present-day dress and the more conventional dress of half a century ago, if only to examine the correlation between dress and the prevailing form or structure of society: whether, for instance, the mass production of clothes of good design, cheap enough for everyone, has caused a blurring of the distinctions; and whether the expendability of most clothes today, compared with their relative permanence at the beginning of the century, has tended towards the same result.

Most of the following account about dress in a middle-class household in a small country town at the beginning of the century comes from Mrs G. Reynolds.[1] She has been intensely interested in dress, and observant of the changes throughout her lifetime. Her account is also an illustration of an important facet of the work of a student of social history. During the past ten years I have had numerous conversations with her, but I was nearly always seeking some specific information that I wanted for my own purposes. But it became clear to me that the subject that Mrs Reynolds herself was chiefly interested in was dress and costume; and simply because it was a lifetime interest, the information she was able to give on this subject was fuller and had in itself the most historical value. The student, therefore, in interviewing old people would be well advised—in addition to searching for the information he hopes to get from his informant—to try and

[1] *The Days That We Have Seen*, pp. 133-9.

tap his or her chief interest. He may well miss something valuable
if he omits to do this. In this connection I recall the complaint of
an old Suffolk shepherd who was interviewed by a man from the
BBC:

'He had a list of questions and I had to answer them. I didn't
have a chance to tell him what *I* wanted to about my job.'

Mrs Reynolds: 'A thing I found frightfully interesting was
watching the mangle being used. Our mangle was about—oh, it
was considerably bigger than a piano. And I shall never forget the
terrible uproar there was because old Mrs Wilkins who used to
come to give a hand with the washing, she was ill; and her
daughter came round. And oh! she put the starched things in the
mangle first. You never heard anything like it! Oh, the tempers
in the kitchen! Every bit of that starch had to be scraped off the
mangle before it could be used for whites, and the sheets and
things. The floor was a mess; and Mother lost her temper which
she seldom did. "Most careless!" And the whole of the morning
was upset over that blessed washing. But, you know, the kitchen
was lovely in the evenings when they did the ironing. There was
the big kitchen-table; and there were the clothes stretched along.
No ironing-boards or anything like that. And you'd have three
people ironing at once; one at the end, and one on each side; and
they'd each got their bits of ironing. And there was some washing
to iron in those days, because Mother used to say:

"However quick you are, you could not do a petticoat with the
goffering under an hour and a half!"

'There were three and a half yards round the bottom of those
petticoats; and then by the time you'd done the ironing then you'd
got to get the pieces at the bottom. You'd got to get the goffering-
irons, get these pieces absolutely straight before you went along
with your goffering-iron. And they came out perfectly lovely. But
it takes a very long time. An hour and half for every petticoat, and
just under an hour for dresses. They had three petticoats each!

'I have an account that I kept of one day in the winter, of what
I was put in; and I don't think I'll ever forget that. It was a thick
woollen vest, and then what was called *stays*: they were made of a
sort of linen, and they had about ten buttons down the front.
And then on there—front, sides and back—there were linen

buttons for your drawers to go on. Well, they reached about an inch below the knees. They also had to be goffered. And we used to beg and implore them not to put starch in because they were so uncomfortable. Then if it was winter-time, over those you'd have your first petticoat. That was usually made of—it was flannelette. Then a real flannel petticoat, luxury! They were very expensive and very nice, and beautifully buttonholed and embroidered round the bottom. That went on top of that. If it was a very cold day they put children into what they called *spencers*. And they came round your neck, with long sleeves down there, skin tight, and dragged over your head. They said they would keep your tummy warm. And so, after that of course, you had your winter-dress put on. It was usually made of merino; that was the material used. It was always made new with two, sometimes three tucks so that each winter the tuck could be let down. If they found it was a red dress and you let it down and it was faded, the braid was always ready to put a strip round. So if you saw a girl coming along with three strips of braid at the bottom of her dress, you knew perfectly well it had been let down three times. Then we used to have the little frills round our necks, and we were allowed those *tuckers* —tuckers they were called. They were put on twice a week; and we'd got to keep our tuckers nice.

'Well, on top of that there was a white pinafore. The pinafores were perfectly delightful: the best pinafores that you put on for tea and that sort of thing. If it was a special occasion, there might be a coloured ribbon on the shoulder. Then there were of course the woollen stockings and the button-boots. And I remember quite well that I had twelve buttons on my boots. And I could see us now sitting down before we went out, and a button would come off and there'd be trouble. The button had to be mended before we went out. There were all those button-hooks in the drawer in the kitchen: we used to quarrel who'd get the best one. Then the coat—you had the pelisse—but coats we used to have as well. But the pelisse was a sort of double cape affair like the old-fashioned coats we used to wear. And that was put on in very cold weather. Then we had a woollen hat or something, pulled down over our ears to keep the east wind off. Then you'd have woollen gloves, and you'd be sent off to school.'

The word *school* induced Mrs Reynolds to digress to tell me her memories of the death of Queen Victoria, a frequent one among people of her age. But it is included here because of the vivid description of the mourning dress of that period:

'But, you know, I'm wandering right away from what I really meant to tell you—and that's about the day when we were just going into prayers in a small, girls' day-school where I was. And, believe it or not, the head-mistress' name was Miss Priscilla Aldwinkle. Suddenly, Margaret and Janet Hooton arrived late; and at the sight of them we all stood with our mouths open. They were dressed in black from head to foot: black dresses with wide crêpe bands, black lace, coats, gloves, stockings, shoes, hair-ribbons; and even their handkerchiefs had black borders. Evelyn Everitt was always the first to speak and said:

"What's the matter?"

'And Margaret Hooton looked at her very solemnly and said:

"Queen Victoria is dead!"

'Well, we all knew that; but we hadn't been told much about it. So when I got home I burst into floods of tears because Mother flatly refused to let me go all in black:

"You can have a black hair-ribbon," she said. But that wasn't any good because my hair was so dark. "And you can have a black band round your arm, and you can wear your black patent leather shoes—but nothing more!"

'The funeral service at the church has left every detail clear in my mind. It was simply lovely. I remember walking slowly between Mother and Daddy. Mother was all in black; Daddy had a band of crêpe around his top-hat with a little bit hanging down the back. The bell was tolling, and the organ was moaning, and every pew was full. And on the wall by the pulpit was a large portrait of the Queen with black velvet draped round the frame. The choir-boys crept along like snails; and the men had little diamond pieces of black cloth sewn into their surplices. I did enjoy watching the ladies trying to get their veils over their hats so that they could cry properly, and not get tangled up. And the men kept coughing and blowing their noses, while the old vicar tried to preach in spite of his crying. The hymns were most beautifully miserable; but I did like the bit in the *Dead March* from *Saul* where it got cheerful. And coming out the sexton was full of foreboding:

"England will never be the same. She purged the courts of Europe!"

'I wanted to run home and tell Maudie all about it; but, of course, I had to walk slowly and wait while different friends discussed the calamity. But at last I got into the kitchen; and there was Ellen, with red eyes, who kept saying she didn't feel up to anything. Until Maudie said that she'd take over; and she told me there was roast chicken for dinner, with all the trimmings, as everybody wanted cheering up. And she told me her young man had said:

"Teddy [Edward VII] would soon put some fireworks under the seats of the old fogies before he was much older!" '

Mrs Reynolds also recalled the clothes worn by the farm-workers at that period in Westerham, particularly those of one workman employed at her home:

'Nobody would believe how perfect some of these men were. Old Henry, for instance; he'd got an old sort of fawnish—what we call now ribbed velvet—corded velvet trousers, tied round the knees with a piece of string (to keep the rats from going up); and he had a smock which was white and I suppose was very old. And she [his wife] had repaired it; because it was all patches and bits and pieces. He had his own—what we call jerkin-sleeves under it. The smock hadn't got sleeves to it. It had a bit of smocking round here [the chest and shoulders], and a huge red and white handkerchief tied round his neck. His jerkin-sleeves were bound with very wide, strong leather; and I can still see his turnip-watch. Now that was the watch Daddy had given him after, I think, the twenty-five years he'd been working for us. Daddy gave him a turnip-watch because he used to look at Daddy's as much as to say:

"Cor! I wouldn't half like a watch like that!"

And he got one. And if he looked at the time once when he was talking to you, he'd look at it twenty times; so everybody could see his watch. And another thing he used to—well, what I thought looked nice—he wore a very old hat with the brim sort of at all angles. But when it was wet, I used to love the way they used to wear those sack head-dresses. You see, they only turned the top of the sack down and pulled it right over, right down over their heads. And the wives used to make big holes in them and tie them round with pieces of string, and a big knot in the front. And it did keep the rain off. The thing that was so interesting in bitterly cold weather was that those head-gears, the sack things that they wore—you could undo them at the bottom if they were going out on a bitterly cold day (there was just the string along like that); and the wives would take that up and put whole sheets of newspaper in. And they'd say:

"He'll never get rheumatism; and he'll never get the cold wind with that on him!"

'I can see Henry now going up with the horses, and having a square of paper pushed right up underneath the clothes he was wearing. They said the north wind could *not* get through that!

'The smock? Of course, his best smock had sleeves to it. Well, I was going down one night to one of the men's cottages—oh, they were nice people—and I was just in time to see what was happening. It was a Saturday night; and of course in the cottages in those days it was *the* great night. And Missus was waiting, and when he took off his smock—they had a long stone sink with a pump at one end; and that sink would have the water pumped into it, and the smocking part of the smock put down into that water to soak for three or four hours. I can still see her now putting that in as he took it off. Of course, I couldn't stay long because right in front of the kitchener there was this large tin bath; and there were enormous kettles ready because it was bath-night. And all his clean clothes were put there ready, everything ready: he'd got his boots polished, and his clean socks, and his great thick combinations that nobody sees now—but they came right down to their ankles, right up to the necks and right down to their wrists; they were warm! Everything was ready to put on, so that when he'd had his supper he'd go down to the pub. I could see the great big cake of soap—it must have been the size of a full bar of Sunlight soap—and a scrubbing brush, and a great coarse towel hanging down by the fire, everything got ready. I knew quite well what was going to happen directly he got out of his bath: the smock was taken out from where it was soaking; it was put into the bath, and there it was left to soak until he was all done up and gone. She'd go down on her knees, and she'd wash that smock; and they got them spotless. Everybody said: "You can't do that if you send them to the laundries!" But they got the smocks like that. They'd had the expense of having the kitchen fire going to get his bath water and everything ready, so she made use of that by just getting this big *horse*—the towel-horse across it. Everybody had one of those nice old-fashioned towel-horses;

93

and his smock would dry by the fire and be ready for Monday morning.

'What was the smock made of? Oh, now—the thickest, what was it called? It was between a canvas and a thick sheeting: there was a special name for it. It wasn't drabbet—not in Kent. Twill, that's it! Twill. But I'll tell you what they did: if they were, well, very poor people they used to do marvellous smocks in thick, unbleached calico. And do you know, they were most attractive because the unbleached calico had flecks of white in it; and I can't tell you how effective that was in those smocks. But I as a child have seen on a winter's day some of the cottage wives with bandages on their fingers: they had been doing smocking with that stuff. With the cold weather, their hands—they'd got their hands in a really bad state through doing, through forcing the needle through this smocking. But I never kept one. Of course they were beautiful to see. These smocks were very warm, too warm in summer. Henry had sleeves in his best one, and also with his smock a thing I found very interesting: I often feel, for the children's sake, I would make one to show them what was done. They had three-cornered pieces of very thick material made of anything —material from the rag-bag. And on the outside of them, they were made with the same colour as the stuff of the smock. They slipped those up over—over the arms and the shoulders, and round the arms there to take the weight of the milk-yoke. The women said that the milking-yoke wore out the shoulders so quickly that they made these pads. They slipped them on, and then they put the yoke on top of them. With them the yoke didn't wear out the smock, and they didn't spoil the look of it at all.

'The aprons of the women in the field: I always thought they were very interesting because if they wanted to keep anything very special they would have an under-pocket. They'd have these pockets in front of their apron to take all sorts of things that they wanted. For instance, if a woman was picking peas or beans and so on and had taken a *carder*[1] with her—or anything like that—she would turn that apron round, and at the back there was a big pocket there, with a button; and things that didn't want to get soiled and wanted taking care of were always put in there. That was her special pocket. Some women had them in their petticoats.

[1] The women always knitted or sewed during rest periods in the fields. They wound their wool round a carder—a specially shaped piece of wood.

My mother did. She had an enormous thing hanging down. And also another thing that was so interesting: the old-fashioned big skirts, and the pockets they had. You used to put all sorts of things in there: I've seen them put all their needlework in a long pocket and put it inside of this pocket, with a button and loop, to carry them. They used the aprons when they were gleaning; and in hay-making time; for instance, when they thought they were going to have their photographs taken or someone was going to see them, it was amazing the number of very nice aprons that suddenly appeared. They'd all take them, and they were lovely.

'Now I have got a dimity[1] pinafore that I wore when I was eight. The only thing that I saved. It isn't one of the pretty fancy ones you wore at parties: it is a working pinafore that we were put in directly we got back from school. Just the workmanship—to look at it now, you can't believe! Quite plain, but my word! couldn't they hem. D'you see, they were taught to do it and to learn it. There were two other things that I have that are rather lovely; one is my husband's christening robe. I think it is about forty babies that have been christened in that robe. One of my brothers-in-law had the sense to put a label on it with the names. I got most of the yellow out of it by soaking it in magnesia. All my grandchildren have been christened in it. Mind you, the modern woman looking at it would simply say: "How could they have darned like it!" It's exquisite. I should think that in that christening robe there are seventeen or eighteen darns, but so lovely you can hardly see them. My husband's family was chris-tened in it; and he was the seventh son. He was eighty-eight when he died, twelve years ago. I suppose it would be about 150 years old.

'And then I've got a photograph [Plate 9] hanging up of my sister at the age of three: that would be about—she died when she was eighty-four, two years ago. And she was being held by a nursemaid of that period—1890?—wearing an embroidered, long —a tiny child's dress; and the maid was wearing a Victorian under-nurse's cap. The people who've seen it—only one person has seen one exactly like it. And she's got this tall sort of cone of lace: the under-nurse always wore that. But I've got another thing in my bag from that period: a vinaigrette which is 200 years old. I can see my grandmother—I admired her!—using it.

[1] A heavy, fine white cotton-fabric with a crimped or ridged surface.

And she used to say—I can see her now (although I was only nine when she died) turning round to me one day and saying to me:

"You know, I take this, dear, when the air wants refreshing. I do *not* have the vapours!"

'I can see her standing up now:

"One thing I want you to remember that your grandmother said to you: Your motto should be *Never be defeated*." '

In one of my conversations with Mrs Reynolds she recollected an incident of her childhood: she had forgotten it until she was reminded of it just before, by seeing a photograph in a recently published book. She had once attended a breeching *(britching)* party when a little boy, after wearing petticoats, was breeched—metamorphosed from a girl into a boy. This was usually done when the child reached the age of four. It would be possible, if not very profitable, to hold forth about this ceremony, and suggest that it was a minor 'rite of passage', a ritualization of a difficult stage in the life of a male child when he was initiated into a different state of 'being'. But this ceremony cannot be compared with the later initiation ceremony at puberty: such a ceremony was world-wide in its celebration, representing a real break in a boy's life when he was separated from his mother and prepared for entry to adult society. The breeching ceremony as described below is a custom that was confined to the upper classes of society, a social custom, helping the child to absorb what was to him a puzzling and uncomfortable rather than a difficult experience. In the breeching ceremony there was no threat of being separated from his mother and his family: he was merely distinguished from her while still remaining in the family. Henceforward he would wear breeches, the symbol in the West—at least until recent years—of the male sex. To convince him that it was not simply the wearing of uncomfortable breeches that was involved, each guest at the ceremony brought him a present to ease the transformation.

Breeching itself was, of course, not confined to one class: it was a natural development in the sense that until a child is continent there would be little point in clothing him in thick garments that would be difficult to wash and dry. Bearing this in mind, the age of four—the recognized time for breeching—appears to be a reasonable age for the change, allowing for the usual regressions after

13 A sailor (*c.* 1895)

14 *The Emperor:* boys wore round hats; girls wore bonnets (*c.* 1890)

the boy is first able to keep himself comfortable. But family custom and individual circumstances often made it much later. There is a photograph, dated 1890, of a group of Warwickshire children of both sexes (Plate 16): all but one are wearing skirts and white pinafores. One of the boys, identifiable by his short hair and boy's cap, is at least seven years old. It is probable that this boy was wearing one of his older sister's clothes; and that the age when most boys were breeched depended not on custom but on the hard fact of whether or not there was a pair of breeches or trousers available for him to get into. It is certain, however, that among the working classes there would be little opportunity or inducement to mark the change with a ceremony. There would probably be no new breeches: a boy would inherit whatever his older brothers had left for him. There would then be no call for a ceremony which would merely put patched necessity on display. The most he would get to mark the occasion would be a ha'penny, or if he was lucky, a penny to put into that new thing—a breeches' or trousers' pocket. Throughout his boyhood he would be compelled to submit to the handing down and making do, perhaps reserving his ultimate revolt for the crisis at puberty when he graduated to long trousers—the *long 'uns* celebrated in the song:

> *Father's pants will soon fit Willy,*
> *Soon fit Willy very well.*
> *Will he wear them: will he wear them?*
> *Will he wear them looking swell?*
> > *Will he wear them?*
> > *Will he wear them?*
> *Will he wear them? Will he—Hell!*
> *Will he wear them? Will he—Hell!*[1]

Breeching as a ceremony confined to the upper classes declined during the nineteenth century. The late Phillis Cunnington wrote:[2] 'I had no idea that the breeching of boys [ceremony] occurred at such a late date as given by Mrs Reynolds [below]. It was usual in the seventeenth, eighteenth and early nineteenth centuries, though not always attended with breeching ceremony. In those

---

[1] Sung in south Wales to the tune of *Cwm Rhondda*.
[2] Personal communication. See also, *Children's Costume in England 1300–1900*, Phillis Cunnington and Anne Buck, A. & C. Black, 1965, pp. 70 ff.

days boys up to the age of four to six wore skirts. They were then breeched and dressed like their fathers in the fashion of the day as far as possible. This was always an important family occasion. Here is a quotation proving this point:

"You cannot beleeve the great concerne that was in the whole family here last Wednesday, it being the day that the taylor was to helpe to dress little Ffrank in his breeches in order to the making an everyday suit by it. Never had any bride that was to be drest upon her wedding night more hands about her, some the legs and some the arms, the taylor butt'ning and others putting on the sword, and so many lookers on that, had I not had a ffinger amongst them, I could not have seen him. When he was quite drest he acted his part as well as any of them, for he desired he might goe downe to inquire for the little gentleman that was there the day before in a black coat [petticoat or tunic], and speak to the men to tell the gentleman when he came from school that here was a gallent with very fine clothes and a sword to have waited upon him and would come againe upon Sunday next. But this was not all, for there was great contrivings while he was dressing who should have the first salute, but he said if old Lane [one edition gives it *Jane*] had been here she should, but he give it to me to quiett them all. They are a very fitt, everything, and he looks taler and prettyer than in his coats [petticoats]. Little Charles reiyoced as much as he did, for he jumpt all the while about him and took notice of everything. I went to Bury and bo't everything for another suitt, which will be finisht upon Saturday, so the coats are to be quite left off upon Sunday. I consider it is not yett terme time, and since you could not have the pleasure of the first sight I have resolved you should have a full relation from

your most affecte Mother

A. NORTH

When he was drest he asked Buckle whether muffs were out of fashion because they had not sent him one."

'This extract is from the Appendix to *The Lives of the Norths*, referring to "little Ffrank at six years old". The date is midseventeenth century. Here is an eighteenth-century quotation: "Boys being in breeches was a convenience in comparison to their wearing frocks or nankeen tunics, which the higher ranks usually kept till their boys were six or seven." The date is 1790—from Mrs Papendiek's Diary 1761–92.'[1]

That breeching was looked upon as an important occasion among the upper classes of early nineteenth-century England we can imply from Charles and Mary Lamb's verses, *Going into Breeches*:

> *Joy to Philip, he this day*
> *Has his long coats cast away,*
> *And (the childish season gone)*
> *Puts the manly breeches on.*

> *Never was there pride, or bliss,*
> *Half so rational as his.*
> *Sashes, frocks, to those that need 'em—*
> *Philip's limbs have got their freedom—*
> *He can run, or he can ride,*
> *And do twenty things beside,*
> *Which his petticoats forbad:*
> *Is he not a happy lad?*[2]

Here is Mrs Reynolds's description of the breeching party she attended in 1901 or 1902 at Westerham in Kent:

'It was at Mrs Edmunds's house. And I so remember the card coming with the invitation to the breeching party, and Mummy saying if I was a very good girl I could go as well. We had formal invitations to the party. They were like the old-fashioned visiting cards; but there were the words *At Home* in the middle, and on the top they'd written *Breeching Party*. Underneath was my mother's name: *Mrs Kelsey—and do bring Baby*. They still called me that when I was that age, ten or more, because I was the youngest.

'And we went over there, and it was really rather wonderful. There was a beautiful tea on the table, all sorts of nice cakes, home made. But Mrs Edmunds wasn't smiling: she was looking rather miserable. It was a very sad day for her; but we didn't think so. At any rate, little Willy was brought in. He was a dear

[1] Mrs Papendiek, *Court and Private Life in the Time of Queen Charlotte*, 1886.
[2] For the full text see *The Oxford Book of Children's Verse*, I. and P. Opie, Oxford, 1973, pp. 145–6.

little boy; he'd got lovely fair curls right down to his shoulders. And she put her hands on his hair and kissed him and made a great fuss of him. Then the maid, Lizzie, came in and whispered to Mrs Edmunds, and we more or less understood it was time for the ceremony to begin. Lizzie put on the side-table, near the tea-table, a pair of scissors, and there was a looking-glass, one of the old-fashioned looking-glasses on a delightful little stand. A large sheet of paper was put there, and Willy was put on a stool. And Mrs Edmunds cut off his curls! They fell down on the paper, and Mother started wiping her eyes; somebody else started crying. I didn't think it was a bit miserable. I thought it was rather fun. All his golden curls were done. Mind you, it did look a bit funny at first until she made it look a bit better. His hair was curly and he looked very nice. And she kept saying: "My poor darling!"

'Anyway, after that Willy was taken behind a screen. He had come in marvellously dressed. As a matter of fact, I've just read Cecil King's autobiography: it was published this year. And there's a photograph of him, at the age of four—the same age as Willy. He's in the most beautiful party-dress. It has puffed lace-sleeves and ribbons, and it's got a full laced skirt and ribbons, and white socks and little girl's shoes. Willy was looking very much like that, not quite so elaborate, perhaps. But he had an enormous blue sash, tied with a bow at the back. There was a screen in the corner of the room, and Willy disappeared behind it; and we heard such a commotion going on behind the screen, and wondered what was going to happen. Well, after about ten minutes Willy appeared. That was the climax. A real little boy!

'But Willy darling wasn't enjoying it. He got kissed all round, and I believe he might perhaps have thought that being a boy now he didn't need it. At any rate, he was put at the place of honour at the tea-table, and we all had a wonderful meal. By this time Mrs Edmunds had at the side of her plate a little packet, and in it were several lockets. She took out one very nice one, and she opened it. It contained quite a lot of hair. Then she said:

"I'm really rather disgusted with George because he thinks I'm not capable of plaiting this hair and placing it into the locket to remember our Willy. He thinks I might take it over to Mr Stacey [the jeweller] because he understands how to do it. He does all the lockets and curls the hair. But I'm determined to have Willy's curls in here."

'After tea Willy was given presents. He was given a top, he was given a hoop, and he had three or four other things. They were all to do with being a boy. And of course all his curls were packed away and put into a box. He was now dressed, as they all were in those days, in a sailor's suit. He was in blue knickers and blue jersey-top, with a wide collar with three white stripes round it, and the big knotted handkerchief in the front. He had a white straw hat that turned up at the brim, with black ribbon round it, and the name of a ship at the front; and two ribbons hanging down the back in black. And he had all sorts of things to do with the sea, a model boat and so on: he was a very lucky little boy.

'Each guest had a lock of Willy's hair, and it was very nicely done. I can see Mrs Edmunds now: she had a little comfit spoon and fork that was always kept on the sideboard for special treats for the children; and she picked up the little pieces of curls with these, so daintily. Then she handed them round to everybody. They were delighted and they put them into their handkerchiefs, or an envelope or a piece of paper. They were all going to take them away. I do remember I was very upset—but I loved Daddy so much; and I always knew when he winked at me that I'd got to keep quiet—for when we got home and Mother put the curls down on the table, saying; "Oh dear! that poor child's curls!" I remember Daddy picking them up and putting them straight into the fire:

"We don't want any more curls here!"

And that was that.'[1]

As implied earlier, the practice of keeping a male child in petticoats and then ceremonially clothing him in his appropriate garments developed as a social custom. Undoubtedly, however, this was a secondary elaboration—merely the husk of the original complex of beliefs, an attempt to supply a rational explanation, or at least a rational-seeming background, in default of the real kernel. It is likely that this is to be sought among that multiplicity of precautions or apotropaic devices which primitives are accustomed to take up in order to avoid provoking the evil influences they believe are always threatening them. These are eager to cancel out anything that looks like good fortune; especially, for instance, a well-favoured child whose parent is rash enough to

[1] For contrast see: Sybil Marshall, *Fenland Chronicle*, Cambridge University Press, p. 226.

boast about him. In Greece up to recent years parents were careulf
—as though still mindful of Niobe's boldness and the retribution
that quickly followed it—not to draw attention to their child's
good graces; and if they did so inadvertently they immediately
covered up with a deprecatory word or formula. Edward Clodd,
the nineteenth-century anthropologist,[1] stated that in India
when several children had died in a family the boys were dressed
as girls to prevent further misfortune; and he draws attention to
Pausanias's reference[2] to the young Achilles who lived among
maidens and was not by his appearance to be distinguished from
them. For when the Greek bands were gathering for the Trojan
War, either Peleus or Thetis—the parents of Achilles—knowing
that he would die at Troy, hid him on the island of Scyros dressed
as a girl. And nearer home: 'To this day the peasants of Achill
Island (on the north-west coast of Ireland) dress their boys as
girls till they are about fourteen years old to deceive "the boy-
seeking devil".'[3]

These observations are confirmed by oral evidence from present-
day Scotland and Ireland where beliefs which are variations of the
above were held until recent years. In Scotland some parents
dressed their children of both sexes in petticoats in their early
years 'to prevent the "little people" stealing the son and heir'.[4]
But it is likely that this custom was more widespread than the
social class that this example suggests, and many sons were kept
in petticoats without any clear reason being adduced for doing so:
it became a social custom that was followed long after its rationale
had been forgotten. In this connection, however, it is an accepted
fact that the male child is more susceptible in his early years to
the various infant diseases than is his sister; and this may well
have helped to give the practice a specious justification. For, given
the old battery of irrational beliefs about the causes of disease, all
of which existed until the comparatively recent formulation of the
germ theory, it would seem a sensible precautionary device to
dress the boy as a girl in order that he would escape the malevolent

---

[1] *Tom Tit Tot: An Essay on Savage Philosophy in Folk-Tale,* London,
1898, pp. 130 ff.

[2] *Description of Greece,* Book 1, Attica, xxii, 6. Loeb Edition, p. 111.
See also R. and E. Blum, *The Dangerous Hour,* London, 1970, p. 341.

[3] Edward Clodd, ibid.

[4] From Michael Brander, Haddington, near Edinburgh.

attention or merely ill-luck that his sister appeared to avoid. Incidentally, this comparative tenderness of the very young male
child is recognized in Ireland by an old folk-saying:

> *Never let a man-child cry:*
> *Never let a man-child long.*

Further oral evidence from Ireland suggests that, whatever the
reason, up to the beginning of this century the time of breeching
was delayed until much later than in Britain.[1] William Egan, born
1898, of Clonfanlough Athlone, when asked about the custom said
that in his time the lads got out of petticoats fairly young—eight
or nine years old. But the generation before his wore them until
they were in their 'teens. He remembered a neighbour named
Kelly, a much older man, who was known to have worn petticoats
until he was fourteen. He was going to school until he was that
age, but not regularly—probably only during the slack time of
winter and early spring: 'And he was coortin' [courting] the girl
he married and he still in petticoats.' A Wexford man of the older
generation: 'I was nearly a man before they put the trousers on
me, and this was so all over Ireland.' A younger man:

'I remember myself when I first had the trousers. I kicked up
an awful din. It took my mother and an aunt of mine to get them
on me. And they only did this after they put tuppence in the
pocket. In the country places a boy would be eight or nine before
he left off petticoats. I recall a rhyme they used to recite not
long ago:

> *Oh, little boy, who made your breeches?*
> *My Mammy cut it out and my Daddy sewed the stitches.*

These suggestions of the primitive origins of the custom of
breeching help perhaps to explain the special and painful involvement mothers had with their young sons who—they believed—
were more under threat than their sisters, especially in certain
environments; and we can better understand their instinctive
reaction to avoid the threat by citing a modern example. Anne
Buck[2] draws attention to one from Germany: 'There is an interesting suggestion, worked out by Walter Havernick of the

---

[1] From James G. Delaney, Hodson Bay, Athlone.
[2] Until recently Keeper of the Gallery of English Costume, Platt Hall,
Manchester. Personal communication.

Hamburg Museum and published in the Museum papers, about the clothing of little boys in Germany before World War 1, that their mothers tried to keep them in short knickers for a longer time as the threat of war grew nearer.' This would tend to persuade us that it was the mother rather than the child who was the emotional centre of whatever ritual there was in the breeching ceremony. She was the one who needed to be reassured and not the 'victim', who apart from the temporary discomfort of his new breeches, would be largely unconscious of what was going on. From the mother's standpoint the child was moving irrevocably— if only a short distance at this stage—out of her immediate orbit; and this would tend to make her sad. Something very similar happens at a child's second dentition when a thoughtful mother might be heard to reflect when the new teeth appear: 'There! Once they have begun to get their second teeth they somehow cease to be children.' This, at least, is how the mother appears to react in the foregoing account of the breeching ceremony.

7
Inside the University

---------------------------------*---------------------------------

Change has swept through the cloisters and corridors of the universities as swiftly as through any other institution, especially since the last war. The universities have been drawn into the process of 'greater production' which appears to be as ineluctable in this field as in any branch of the economy. They have increased in number and size; and have been geared more and more to the 'nation's demands', that is more directly to commerce and industry. A little of their character before expansion can be gathered from the following account by an outspoken and observant lady who was head of the Catering Department of a provincial university forty years ago. Miss Meg G. Masson, who is of Scottish descent, was born in Kent in 1894:

'I was in charge of the catering at the National Physical Laboratory at Teddington: this was in the early 'thirties. And one day one of the Senior Scientific Officers drew my attention to an advertisement in the Public Appointments columns of *The Times*. It was for a similar job to the one I was doing—at the University of Leeds; and on his suggestion I applied. Well, after the usual formalities, two or three interviews and so on, I got the job; and I went up to Leeds in 1935.

'It amused me greatly to think I was to be the head of an administrative department of a university. Yes, I did the catering for the whole University: I ran the refectory for the students, and did the socials and dinners for the many societies, the catering for the Entertainments Committee. Later I did the catering for the Council and the Senate; and later still I had charge of the cafeteria in the students' union. (I was responsible to the students for that. I had a man as a general manager, and his wife worked with him. I engaged the staff for that; and I also looked after the financial part and did the buying. When the war broke out we had a night staff as well.) It was a very varied job: I really needed to cut myself in three; then I could have got along very well!

'When I went there, the buildings were for the great part the original buildings: pseudo-Gothic. But the University had a very big building programme; and it was buying up property—houses, anything they could lay hands on; demolishing them in order to prepare for the rebuilding. This, of course, got badly held up by the war. Some private houses they left; and these were used for the Departments, with the University increasing very much in size (there were 1,700 students when I was there). Had the war not taken place they would have gone straight ahead with their building scheme. Even so, the new library was built with money that had been left them by Lord Brotherton; that was completed while I was there. When I arrived they had dismissed everybody. They wished me to start afresh; they wanted a new approach entirely. I was asked to do that; and I myself was determined to have model kitchens. (Later, deputations from other universities used to come to see my kitchens.) I was also asked to prepare a financial scheme. I told them when I was being interviewed that I was very bad at arithmetic; and it would be unfair to them to engage me, not realizing that. But they brushed that aside and said:

"Oh, the Accounts Department will keep you on the rails."

'Compared with many of the professors and the Staff of the University I later found that I passed un-noticed! Well, I worked out my scheme, and it was adopted by the Accounts Department; and it was in operation all the time I was there.

'I had to engage my staff myself. Nobody knew how many I'd got, or what they were paid. That was the beginning of my fight to get things on a sound footing, and an *honest* footing; because as far as my building was concerned, it was riddled with dishonesty from top to bottom. And the first thing I did was to get a chef. When I proposed this, I was sent for by the Vice-Chancellor who thought it was a very bad idea. I asked him, why? He hadn't any real reason except that they had never had one before!—There's a general view of chefs that they are extravagant. But they're not! They are much, much more thrifty than the best housewife. They may use extravagant materials in their cooking; but nothing is wasted—ever. They use the outside of the cabbage leaves, for instance; and even the heads and tails of shrimps are mortared down and passed through a sieve and made into shrimp-paste. Oh yes, very thrifty! I was fortunate in getting a chef who was really an artist at his work; and he and I worked together to get the place straight.

'For example, when you buy meat by the hundredweight, as we did—whole carcasses of mutton, a quarter of a carcass of beef—the butcher would bring it to the kitchen: you had no means of knowing whether the weights were accurate. So the first thing I did was to buy one of those platform, yard-arm scales you used to see on railway-stations. The kitchen was upstairs; and the butcher was made to put the meat on the scales at the bottom of the stairs; and the chef would go down to him. He would check the weight before anything was done. But even with an honest chef, the trades-people would approach him and offer him presents. And I had to deal with them; I had to go to them and say:

"If you do anything of that sort, or offer my chef bribes in any shape or form, I won't have my meat from you—or I won't have my fish from you!"—whatever it was.

'And if necessary, I *would* break with them. So they were all on their toes. That was the first step we made to put things right. Then I had the three store-rooms locked; appointed a store-keeper; and began stock-taking at regular intervals. But I never got rid of pilfering!

'You see, at the end of the session we had a three months' vacation. We couldn't afford to keep the whole staff through the vacation. We just kept a key-staff, and all the rest were dismissed. So before the autumn term began, I had to go back to Leeds about a fortnight before term started; and I had to engage people as fast as I could get them. If you engaged them too early, they'd drop out if there was no work for them to do, even if you paid them! Drop out and get other jobs. So you couldn't leave it too long. Some would apply and they would come for re-engagement; others were new. Towards the end of my time at the University I used to engage everyone who was likely, even though I engaged more than I needed; because there was always a drop-out when they began to do the work. My heart used to sink when I looked at the staff at the beginning of the session, knowing they'd got to be licked into shape. I never got over that problem. Occasionally, though, we did have conferences in the summer vacation—oh, I must tell you this: it's a digression but it's rather funny.

'They were concerned about the atmosphere in Leeds; and *The Smoke Abatement Society* came up and had a big conference there. Before I arrived at the University they had rebuilt the physics laboratory; and there were physics, chemistry and organic chemistry on three separate floors. And this conference was held on the top floor; and one side of the big laboratory was all glass. And it looked straight out onto the top of a great chimney which was belching out black smoke from the University central-heating plant. Everyone in the University was much amused by this: the conference had a fine view of the problem! Someone in the University had been doing research-work into the atmosphere of Leeds which was very bad at that time; and it was reported that there was enough lethal stuff in the air to practically kill the lot of us! It was awful. I suppose it was mainly sulphuric acid. Leeds was a very dirty place. There was a women's hall I stayed in until I got a flat. There they had forty study-bedrooms for the students; there were also the warden's sitting-room and bedroom; there was the sub-warden's and there was the matron's bed-sitting room. And every one of these had a coal-fire! And the wretched servants had to fetch the coals and light the fires and do the grates every morning. Best household coal was then twenty-one shillings a ton. It was quite Victorian! But domestic labour was still very cheap.

'But to go back to the refectory and the staff. I got so experienced with staff that I more or less knew, when my office-door opened and someone appeared round it for an interview, that I could size them up. I knew exactly what they were good for; and I knew where I should have to watch out; where I should have difficulties (there were never enough good ones!). And I even got to the stage where I could tell a certain type of dishonest person—not every kind of dishonest person; but some of them I could put my finger on. The kind that I can spot is the ones that are too pleasant. I know them at once: I suspect them at once. When I first was let down by that type of person I couldn't believe it! But latterly I got to know it when I saw it. But there are other kinds of dishonesty that I couldn't spot; and I nearly always shipped about one dishonest person at the beginning of the new session. It was an awful nuisance; because when the University opened it was such a busy time—the new students, and all the societies were trying to get the students to join their particular society, so that to have to go tracking a thief was the last straw. It took time; but I got quite expert at it.

'There was always so much food about; and the staff thought

that the University could afford it. And it was not only the domestic staff. I did some very thorough investigation and found it was also rife in the maintenance staff. They had a farm attached to the University, just outside York. We used to buy potatoes by the ton; and they used to be tipped into great bins we had down in the lower kitchens. There were no means of checking them at all. And the man used to come with the lorry from the farm—Askham Bryan. The Refectory Committee thought it was an awfully good idea to have green stuff and vegetables from Askham Bryan; and they recommended this procedure. But, you see, it wasn't a good idea! Because when I rang up for potatoes they'd say:

"Well, the weather is too hard: we can't open the clamps."

'I couldn't do with that sort of thing. But for some time I had given instructions to my staff that I wished to be informed when the man came from the farm as I wanted to go down and check the potatoes. They would not: they absolutely wouldn't do it! They would come up to my office and say:

"The potatoes have come."

'And I'd say: "Where's the man?"

"Gone."

"I thought I told you that I wanted to be informed when they came. If you won't check them, I must check them."

"Well, he's gone!"

'This went on for some time; and I couldn't make headway at all. At last they came up and said:

"Potatoes have come."

"Where's the man?"

"Gone."

'So I went downstairs; and by this time I had got them to leave the potatoes in sacks; so at least I could count the sacks. The man *had* gone. The potatoes were there in the sacks; and there was one missing—nineteen instead of twenty. So I went to the back-door; and there was the lorry outside still; and the man was doing something to the engine. It was a bitterly cold day. But I flew after him and said:

"You haven't left the right number of sacks. There's one sack missing."

"No! I left the right number."

'(They always argue in Leeds!) So I said:

"Well, what's that sack doing there?"

"Oh . . . that's . . . I've got to deliver it somewhere else."

'So I said: "Well, you can just come back and count these sacks with me."

'And I made him come back with me; and we counted the sacks; and of course there were only nineteen. So I said:

"That sack in your lorry belongs to me. I'll have it in, please." And he brought it in.

'Later, I rang up Askham Bryan and reported this; and they said:

"Oh, our man wouldn't do a thing like that! Oh no! he's perfectly honest. He's been working with us for years."

'But that finished Askham Bryan as far as I was concerned: I wouldn't have them again.

'Ceremonial functions: that was the most interesting part of my work, really. For one of these dinners it used to take the dining-room staff a whole afternoon to lay the tables out. And the gold-plate had to be got out, a fearful performance. It used to come up in—you know those bakers' baskets on wheels—well, it used to come up in those; and it had to be kept in the University in a special safe because of the insurance. And there was far more of it than we could ever put on the tables. We used to have about fifty people at a time for these dinners, fifty visitors; and each professor would take a visitor and be his host for the evening. (I could tell you more than a quarter of an inch of tape about what used to happen at these dinners.) They were very interesting. The chef used to enjoy it very much because he could really spread himself. I never refused the chef anything he wanted. And he used to make his famous turtle-soup. It would take him three days to make it; and he used to come sidling up to me and say:

"I wonder if I could have just two pounds of fillet of veal for my turtle-soup."

'But I always gave him his fillet of veal—which was rather an extravagance, in one way, for turtle-soup.

'Now when we had these dinners, people used to ring me up; and they'd tell me they'd had an invitation to the dinner that was going to take place at the end of the week: *What was the catch in it?* And so I used to get out my best official, university manner; and I used to say that the Entertainments Committee thought it was only right that important inhabitants of Leeds should know something about the University, and the work that went on there. But the real *catch* was money! The University didn't mind who it was. Once a year, we had the Lord Mayor; and the chauffeur who drove the Daimler car, year after year, was infinitely superior to the average Lord Mayor. And on one occasion we had a Lord Mayor who didn't arrive on time. We had given this Lord Mayor up and started the meal; but he came, half an hour late. And he sat down at the table and started at the beginning! That was another mistake because if you're late at a dinner, you start and go on from the point that the dinner has reached. But no, he started at the beginning: hors-d'œuvres, soup, fish—and he held the whole dinner up, and the guests had to wait for him. He finished up with an orange, and he shouted over his shoulder for a spoon. So a teaspoon was brought him on a tray; and then he proceeded to attack the orange with this teaspoon. When the waitress cleared away later there was a whole ring of juice on the table cloth.

'Now the wines at these dinners used to bother me a little when I first went there. But Miss Selby, the Vice-Chancellor's secretary, told me:

"Now if you would take my advice, I know of a very good wine-merchant—a father and two sons—in the town. They really know about wines; and they'll advise you."

'And I was quite pleased because I didn't know a great deal about wines. So I went to this father-and-sons business; and they were very helpful to me throughout. If I had a very important dinner, I would go down to their wine-shop and show them the menu and tell them: "We've got this dinner; and we've got these people . . ." The University always had a *bait* there in the form of —it might be Lord Harewood, or Lord Birdwood, or the Chancellor—the Duke of Devonshire. It might be anybody they could lay hands on in order to entice people to accept the invitation and come to the dinner; and they would be introduced to *them*, you see. *They* knew all right! The important guests, I mean. But the wine-merchant would say:

"Oh yes, Lord Harewood. He's very fond of such-and-such a wine."

'(They all knew Professor *Ham Tom* [Hamilton Thompson], too. He had the top drawer of his desk full—it was like a wine-cellar. He was fond of claret—a certain vintage.) They would ring me up and say:

"We've got some sherries in. If you'd like to come down, we shall be tasting them this afternoon."

'And they'd let me try the sherries; and I'd tell them what I thought; and they'd tell me what I ought to have thought! But I did learn quite a lot that way.

'When we had a ball we used to take wines down to the main University in those great big laundry baskets with iron hasps and straps and padlocks. And they used to be locked in a room when we'd finished, with a double master-key because we had to have a van next day to take all the stuff back: we had to wait till next day before we could get the van again. And then, even though the basket was padlocked and the room locked, we would find something missing! I couldn't understand it because those baskets are very stiff, you know. Well, it was curious that sometimes only a bottle of soda-water would be gone, and then a bottle of wine. Funny that, if they were after wine, they should take soda-water! And then I found that you could get your hand in at the corner and grab (it rather hurt your hand) whatever was there. So that is why they took soda-water sometimes: it was in the corner! So I bought some mouse-traps; and I set them at each corner of the basket—without any bait on! And when they went next day they had gone off. I was very pleased about that. But I went down to the secretary of my committee and I told him about this. He was a funny little man, and he sat looking at the table; and I thought: He's going to disapprove of this very much. He looked up:

"Would it mark their fingers when the trap went off?"

'So I said:

"Well, I let one off on my thumb when I was setting the trap. Look! it doesn't show, does it? But I imagine they'd have a very sore thumb!"

'He looked down at the table again; and he turned it over in his mind; and he looked up again and said:

"Pity you didn't put rat-traps there!"

'More about the wines and so on: The Duke of Devonshire was the Chancellor. The old Duke was there when I first went to Leeds; and then his son became Chancellor in his place. He was a man about my own age, and a terrific drinker. I never saw a man drink like him and still keep sober—although his stories would get near the knuckle. But on one occasion when I sent the bill to the University for what he had one night, they wouldn't believe it!

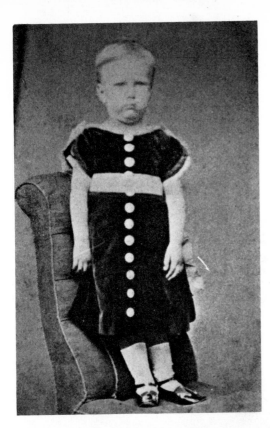

15 Boy just before breeching:
C. E. Reynolds, born
19.x.1875

16 Country boys in petticoats

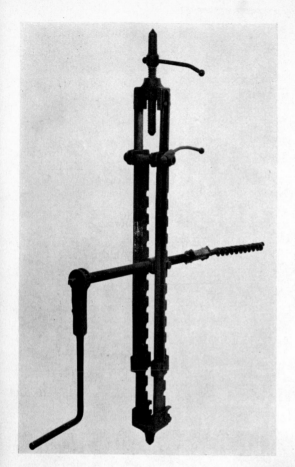

17 Top-machine: for boring holes in the rock above the coal seam, ready for firing

18 Curling-box: for lifting coal or *rubbish* off the ground

They sent for me. And he'd had—now if I remember: he started off with sherry; and then he had white wine with the first part of the meal; and he'd had that—I think he had a whole bottle to himself because he was guest of honour. Then he had a bottle of red wine. Then he had port and liqueurs. Then he went into the reception room with the port decanter, and had whisky for the rest of the evening. The Vice-Chancellor at that time was Mouat Jones. He was a bachelor and lived in a very big house; and the Duke stayed with him that night. And the Vice-Chancellor complained next day that the Duke had finished all his whisky! When I sent the bill in for what he'd drunk at the dinner, they thought: No, no! he couldn't have drunk all that! But when I went down and told them, they were interested and quite believed me. He got very talkative; but otherwise he was all right.

'Apropos the Chancellor: I was, I suppose, very fortunate to see his Installation ceremony. This doesn't happen very often. But the old Duke had died and his son, the new Duke, had accepted an invitation to take his place. I used to think that Leeds, a very rich university, was incredibly mean in many ways, but would spend money like water on other occasions. And this was one of them. This event involved them in a week of junketings. My memories of the Installation itself are rather vague now, but I remember the Duke outside the Town Hall door, knocking to be admitted; and a deputation of distinguished people from the platform (the pro-Vice-Chancellor was with them) making a solemn procession the length of the Hall. Then they opened the door and admitted the Duke and escorted him to the platform where they proceeded to confer on him an honorary degree. But before this is done a lengthy and very dull screed is read out, listing the outstanding events and achievements of his life. The students seek to liven things up a bit by interruptions and the throwing of paper-darts. Eventually the new hood is put over his shoulders.

'But my thoughts were far away; for I had 2,000 people coming to a buffet supper that evening. We had eight supper rooms dotted about the University; and I put senior members of my staff in charge of each room, and supplemented these with the remainder and others borrowed for the evening from the men's and women's Halls of Residence, and from the Medical School. This is not difficult work to arrange, but one must see to it that nothing is forgotten. A missing corkscrew or even a drawing-pin will dislocate the smooth running of the arrangements. But before the guests were let loose in the supper rooms I had to change into some "glad rags" and go and be *presented* in the Great Hall of the University, escaping down the back-stairs immediately afterwards to continue supervising.

'The guests certainly did justice to the food: some of them went from room to room stoking up; and I don't think they could have seen much of the University which was on view. Then one of the professors asked me whether I'd had anything to eat, and took me along to the main supper room for the specially invited guests. This room had been decorated by a down-town florist and was—it was unrecognizable. The Duke and the Duchess were sitting by the fire, and I sat down and joined in. The Duchess was wearing a tiara. It sparkled with colour and danced like fire. I had never seen a tiara *in situ* before and I have never seen one since. But I was still working and had to leave. Shortly after this, a little man was brought to me: he'd had nothing to eat all day (he'd had plenty to drink!). As the staff were all occupied I took him to the night-watchmen's refectory where the university porters, electricians, plumbers and joiners were being fed. This man belonged to Ede and Ravenscroft from Chancery Lane in London. They house the regalia until it is wanted. It is then sent out in large laundry baskets. A man is sent with them; and it's his duty to see that they are worn correctly. We were talking about the Coronation as we walked, and I mentioned that I had handled a small piece of silk from which the Queen's (now the Queen Mother) gown had been made. He told me that she'd *not* had a new purple velvet (edged with miniver) cloak, but had worn Queen Victoria's which had been adapted to fit her. He asked me if I would like a piece of the velvet. I looked at him and thought to myself: "He will have forgotten all about this offer tomorrow." But no! in due course I received my small piece of Queen Victoria's velvet cloak; and I have it still.

'As far as I know there were no students present at this event—which seemed to be a pity. The students had a Ball to themselves (about a thousand strong) on the next night. I always felt that the students were excluded from the most colourful events in the University which, in the main, were arranged for the University staff. The students were very lively, of course. I remember on one occasion a student dropped something under the table and crawled underneath to retrieve it. Almost at once, the rest of the students at that table joined him; and the table began to career down the dining-room, lurching from side to side. I still smile when I remember the sight of my head-waitress—a very dignified woman—looking very displeased as she followed the table round, collecting cutlery and glass before it was smashed.

'The engineering students were the ones who locked me in my office with the Vice-Chancellor. The old gentleman plucked at the handle of the door and couldn't get it open; and I went to see what was the matter and found that we were locked in. They had taken all the bulbs out of the electric light points outside my door and the main door to the stairs entrance. But what they didn't know was that I had a master-key. And there was another exit, and I was able to get the old gentleman out.

'The engineering students were very lively, but they were nicely lively. I never minded what they did. I knew who'd done this. You see you always get one group working throughout the year; and you soon get to know who they are. In this case I ran into what I was fairly sure was the ring-leader. I had to bluff very often; so I said to him:

"It was unfortunate for you it was the Vice-Chancellor who was with me when you locked me in my office."

'They all looked so innocent; they looked too innocent, you know, as if they didn't know what I was talking about.

"You remember," I said, "when you locked me in the office the other day: I had the Vice-Chancellor with me." And I said: "It was unlucky for you it was the Vice-Chancellor."

"Oh! Why?"

"You go down and ask him: he'll tell you!" So I said: "If you allow me to give you a little advice, I'd put those electric bulbs back."

'And—I don't know when they did it—but quite shortly afterwards they were all back. You had to bluff sometimes.'

'It's interesting, you know, that the professors are quite as anxious about examinations as the students are—did I tell you about this? Professor Comber came to see me one day and said:

"I've got an Examiner coming from Cambridge; and I and my

staff thought we would like to give him a dinner. Could you do it?"

'I said I could; and he went on:

"This man's got a duodenal ulcer; and we thought we'd better put a dinner on that's suitable. Could you do a duodenal ulcer dinner?"

'I said we could do that. So after he'd gone I got the chef in and we sat down and worked out a dinner with everything that was right and light—that couldn't possibly hurt a duodenal ulcer.

'When the evening came we had the dinner in the professors' room which was attached to my refectory. After they arrived Professor Comber sent a message to my office to ask me to come and be introduced to their guest. After I'd met him, the Examiner asked me if he could have a wineglass of olive oil. When it arrived I watched him with horror as he drank the whole glassful. The others were having sherry. So they sat down at table and the dinner began. Then Professor Comber asked him what he would care to drink from the wines. He said: if we didn't mind, he'd have milk! And out of courtesy all the others ordered milk and continued to drink milk throughout the evening. We had a fair amount of milk in every day; but we didn't allow for a situation like that; and we had to send down and knock up a dairy in the city. But they finished the dinner; and Professor Comber came and thanked me.

'Well, a year went past, and Professor Comber came to see me again; and he said:

"I say, we've got that Examiner coming here again!"

'So I said: "How is his duodenal ulcer?"

"Well, he didn't say anything about it. I think it's better. But he's still got it."

'So we set about planning another special dinner; and this time I saw to it that there was plenty of milk in, and olive oil! On this occasion Professor Comber brought his visitor and introduced him before the meal; and I asked him:

"How is the duodenal ulcer?"

He said: "Fancy you remembering that!"

'The chef left towards the end of my reign there; and then I had a lady-cook. She used to have her own sitting-room, a fire lighted for her every day, and two people to carry down her meal and wait on her while she was eating. (Miss Masson only had one maid; and that one did everything, including lighting the fire.) There's a fearful hierarchy among your staff, you know; and you can't break it. Your head staff won't have meals with the lower grade staff; and the kitchen staff won't have truck with anybody. They are fearful snobs.

'Well, the chef—we got along very happily until his mother died, and he was left some money. And that money burned a hole in his pocket, and he became hoity-toity. He became restless; and I knew until that money was spent, that I wouldn't be able to do much with him. And he finally decided he was going to open a cake-shop at Otley, not very far away. He came and told me; and I said:

"That won't work," I said.

"Why not?" he said.

"Because you're far too peppery. The first time a customer is *trying* in your shop, you'll come out and order her out of the shop. You won't think twice about it. You'll ruin any shop in six months!"

'But he left and took my second-best cook with him. They were living together by that time. He had a wife; his wife used to come and stay with them sometimes; and the whole three of them used to take tea with me. But we were quite used to that at that period. But the chef was an artist and could do beautiful work. But—I remember on one occasion: Yorkshire people are passionately fond of dried peas. They have funny tastes; and swedes are another thing they love. (They won't eat them here [in East Anglia]: turnips they will eat but never swedes.) And every hundredweight bag of dried peas that you cooked needed a different time to cook. Some of them cooked more quickly than others; and they were always done in the steam-oven. Anyway, on this occasion I went through the kitchen to get to the dining-rooms; and the peas evidently weren't cooked; and the time for the meal had started; and the chef was laying into his head vegetable-cook:

"Can't cook a few bloody peas!"

'So I didn't *hear* this; and I said:

"Aren't the peas ready?" So to my next-in-command I said: "Take my keys, and go down to the store-room and bring up some tinned peas; and we'll start with those."

'It was very expensive for students' lunches; but it kept the thing going; and we started like that. And when I thought the peas had been in the steamer long enough; and I thought my peas were going down too quickly, I went through to the kitchen, and I said to the chef:

"Do you think, Chef, those bloody peas are ready now?"

'Of course, where the staff had been all red in the face there were huge grins, and the chef looking very silly.

'But there was always something interesting going on; and I had an inside view of all the rivalries and jealousies among the staff—teaching, administrative and maintenance. It was easy, too, to see the funny side of the pomp and self-importance of some of the townspeople. But the war came along, and things got hectic. I was getting badly overworked; in fact, the job wanted someone more robust than I was at the time. With the extra burden of a hundred all-night fire-watchers, and the University Training Corps who worked throughout the vacations, life got too full. It was at this time that I gave place to a successor (I'd been training her for some while) and I left to take up work in the country where I'd been bred and born.'

Part Two
Industry: Mining

———————*———————

8

Miners and Mining

———————————— ✳ ————————————

My first introduction to the idea of collecting oral evidence
was in the early 1930s. This was in the mining valleys of Glamorgan where I was born and brought up. I had graduated in 1930
and I left university in the following year, a few weeks before the
economic collapse. This was quickly followed by a cut of ten per
cent in all Government salaries—civil servants, police, teachers
and so on—and a savage depression of wages all round. Many
graduates found themselves in an economic no-man's land. There
was a big retraction in the spending of the education authorities;
and teaching jobs—particularly specialist ones—were not easy to
get. Graduates who had specialized hung on, hoping for the
position to change: instead it worsened. There was no 'social
security' in the sense that we have come to know it today. Anyone
who had completed professional training and was waiting for a
job could not qualify even for the meagre *dole* of that time,
the theory being, no doubt, that since you had never done any
work you could not, therefore, be out of work and qualify for
the dole. Whoever was in this position, whatever the logic of it,
had to live as best he could, usually it was on the charity of his
parents.

It was during this period of unemployment that I started to
write; and like many who have begun without any counsel or
present example I floundered about in some very shallow waters.
I recall, however, that I got my greatest satisfaction at this time
through translating short lyrics of classical authors—chiefly
Horace and Catullus—into English verse. Although some were
printed they hardly improved my position.

Later, I began to write short stories and came nearer to earth
by using the background I knew: the mining valleys and particularly the miners. My immediate neighbours were miners; and in
my walks on the hills, eating up time and taking the free air, I had

often met groups of miners going along the old Roman road that ran along the spine of the hill above my home. If there was a cool breeze I would sometimes find them squatting on the lee side of a dry-stone wall. Here, almost any topic under the sun was likely to be tossed about in the course of a morning's talk. Sometimes there were only a couple of men 'up on the mountain'; sometimes there were as many as half a dozen sheltering under the wall. Some were unemployed, some disabled by pneumoconiosis (collier's lung); and one or two were still working, but on the night-shift which left their morning or afternoon free. I recall the occasional sunny day when the stone wall became warm with a welcome heat, and the talk was lightened by a dry humour and saving bursts of laughter. But as I look back, most of the days were grey, with the surrounding hills withdrawn, inscrutable presences, the silence broken by the plaintive bleating of sheep, or their scuffling and sudden bedraggled appearances out of the mist.

The state of the nation was inevitably one of the major themes of the talk on the hills at that period; but so also was the change that was taking place rapidly in the collieries of the steam-coal areas where work was being 'rationalized', a much-used euphemism for the cutting of labour costs. Although ventilation of the mines (by huge steam-driven fans) and haulage (the raising and lowering of the cage or lift in the deep mines, and much of the transport underground) had long been mechanized, work at the actual coal-face was still done by hand in many collieries; and pit-ponies still dragged the small four-wheeled *drams*—the tubs or trams from the working places to link up with the mechanized 'journeys'. Up to this period, mining had been essentially a handcraft where, as in farming, man-power and horse-power had been the chief means of winning the product. This hand-craft stage was characterized by the *stall system*. In the stall method of working, a collier and his helper—the boy—worked a limited space of the coal-face with the old hand-tools: the mandril or pick, the shovel, the hand boring-set and the axe for cutting the timber that supported the roof. Now, the mechanical coal-cutter, the conveyor belt, and the steel arch for roof support were quickly supplanting the old hand-methods, and for the stalls were substituting the long face where the coal-cutter undercut a greater length of the coal-seam, and the colliers, instead of working in pairs, now worked in groups, filling the coal onto the moving conveyor belt that ran parallel to the face.

It was these long discussions about the new working conditions, as well as the humour and the well-informed and perceptive comments on the politics of the time, that interested me greatly; and I spent a whole shift and part of a shift respectively in two mines near my home—the *Deep Navigation* at Abercynon and the *Ocean* at Ynysybwl—in order to understand some of the workings and to get the atmosphere of *underground* which I later used as background to some of the stories I was writing.

Among the miners on Gilfach-yr-hydd hill one of the chief objections to the new system that was coming in was the noise that the machinery made. 'It's like Hell there now!' was a frequent comment. For the early conveyors were not the more or less noise-less rubber-belts they are using today, but long metal structures made up of sections of shallow pans which moved the coal forward by a series of spasmodic jerks. The *jigger* the men called it. And what they feared most was that the noise made by the machines would mask the faint warning sounds that came before any movement of the *top*, the roof above the roadway or the working place. In the quiet of the stall where there were no sounds except those made by themselves, a barely heard *crack* or a faint trickle of dust from the roof would warn them they must take some action: either put up more support timber or, if they interpreted the warning sound more urgently, move quickly out of danger before the roof fell down or the place caved in. With mechanization, therefore, there was an inevitable increase in the tension of working. But the noise and the new stress were only the first, obvious effects of the change: later, as some of the older miners quickly realized, the change went much deeper. The coming of the machines to the coal-face basically changed the underground work-force in mining. There had been a drastic change in the character of the work; and this argued a corresponding change in the whole social climate of mining.

This was the effect I had posited in my researches into farming in East Anglia. In that region there appeared to be a direct, organic relation between the old type of arable farming, which relied chiefly on man and the horse, and the traditional society which this farming had nourished. When, therefore, farming became fully mechanized it not only revolutionized techniques on the farm itself but became the chief agent of change in rural society. What were the specific effects of mechanization on mining and the mining community? To follow this question right through would, I was well aware, mean years of work and innumerable conversations with old miners. I could not do this; but at least I could return to Glamorgan and find out from miners who worked under the old stall-system whether or not I was asking the right question. I returned in June 1973.

I went back to Mountain Ash where I had been at school, and I met the brother of one of my school-fellows, Jack Evans. He had started work in the mines as a boy, but had left about fifteen years later during the depression of the early 'thirties. He had experienced the change-over from stall-work to mechanization which came after the First World War. His generation, too, as he reveals, were often the children of those men who came into the coal-valleys from the country to look for work after the pits had been sunk. In Mountain Ash the first mine was opened in 1850,[1] but the big invasion of the Aberdare valley did not begin until later when additional and deeper mines were opened. In 1864 Mountain Ash was a small village but by 1911 its population had risen to well over 40,000. Jack Evans told me:

'I was born in 1901 in a place called Rhydlewis in Cardiganshire. I came up here when I was three years old. My father came up here to work in the mines; my mother died in Rhydlewis and I came up here with my father. I went to Darranlas school till I was fourteen. In February 1915 I started in the mines on my first shift. I was fourteen in the morning, and I went to work that night. I went there as a boy. Well, what could I do? Carry a lamp that was dragging on the floor, very near, as I was going in because I was so short. Well, the men—they told me:

"You put that coal into that tub by there; and after you've done, you have a little spell till I'm ready for you again."

'That was my first night underground; and when I came home in the morning, I was very tired. Every penny counted in those days. I was having twelve shillings a week. That was my wages: six days a week, Monday to Saturday.

'I didn't think very much of it. I was frightened, I'll say that, first of all when I went into the face because seeing everything in

[1] William Bevan, *Hanes Aberpennar* [The History of Mountain Ash], H. Humphreys, Caernarfon, 1897.

front of you in darkness and only this little oil-lamp I had going in, and naturally it was a bit frightening. I had a little box of food, a tommy-box it was called, and a little tin jack of water. That was the standard equipment for a collier at that time, with the Davey lamp. No electrical lamps, no cap-lamp. The collier I went with was a gentleman from Dyffryn Street here. I went to see him, and went with him that night. He was a very good man, one of the best mates you could have had. As you went and you got to know the men better, you enjoyed it as far as things were at that time, because there was no other work about. Only the mines was all that was in front of everybody at that time; and everybody working from the oldest son to get a wage, to earn a couple of coppers to help things at home—especially if there was a large family. You had to find it then.

'At that time it was done with no machinery. The mandril, the shovel and the curling-box[1]—these were your tools. I was working in a seam that was roughly two feet six inches high. Your mate would send you to the top end of where you were working; you'd have to drag this curling-box of coal down; and take the curling-box of muck back up to keep filling in behind you. The coal went into the tub or *dram*; and the rubbish into the place to pack behind you for safety—to help keep the roof up. What they called the *gob*, at that time.

'Later on, when I went to work with my father, he taught me how to notch the timbers and put them up. After then, when I finished with my father, I went on the coal-cutting machine. That was a different system. That was a different system altogether from a mandril and shovel. The coal-cutters came in about 1918—that's when I think they started on 'em myself. At least that's when I went on them first. How long they had been going before then I can't tell you. The conveyor troughs came in later: I went on them in 1924. I never had a collier's stall on my own. I went onto the coal-cutters, and stopped on the coal-cutters until I finished in the mines in 1930. The system was changing while I worked there from the stall-system to mechanization. Which did I prefer? Well, for the easiest it's the conveyors, isn't it? You take a man going in there, lying on his side, heaving the coal out and putting it on the dram. Today you got machines cutting it and loading it for you. That's the difference in the systems. But there's

[1] See later p. 140; also Plate 18.

another side: in the stall-system every man had a pride in his work. Today, it's cut the coal, chuck it to one side, move on. Rip it out. As long as it is going out it is all right. In the old system, every man had his pride: "Keep my place as clean as I can, and try and get it as good as the man next up to me." You take the system today; in the old days you'd have a dram of coal; the dram was filled; then you had what they called *racing*, the coal built up around the edge of the dram with pieces of timber, the length of a man's arm, you could say, above the lip of the dram. What happens today? You're only getting a bare dram of coal which is three parts small coal. It was all large coal then: a man wasn't getting paid for his small coal in those days. Mining was a craft at that time.'

Perhaps it would be as well to anticipate a later chapter here, and to include a note describing the *racing* of a dram of coal in the anthracite district. Douglas Miller, who worked in one of the mines in the upper Dulais valley in the 'thirties, writes:

'With us, where the coal is harder, a wall of coal about a foot high was built above the level of the top of the dram. No timber was used, and I remember the contempt natives felt for those who came from the other part of the coal-field. Our chaps took a pride in the neatness with which they carried out the job of putting the maximum amount of coal into a dram without running the risk of having any brushed off or lost. (If it was too high, it could come into contact with a low tunnel roof somewhere on its journey to be weighed on the surface.) There was a chap from Merthyr in the stall next to the one I once worked in: he didn't know how to race a dram! You couldn't belong until you mastered this technique.'

But to return to Jack Evans:

'When I started the men wouldn't tell you much. You had to pick that up for yourself. But they'd tell you the dangers, mind you: "Watch whatever you're doing. When you are coming out and there's a rope working" (which you shouldn't be doing to start with!) "look out for it." They'd tell you all the dangers that were expected down below—unforeseen dangers. If you dropped your lamp and it went out, then you'd have to get your mate's lamp and go back to the *locking-hole*, where the fireman was, and have it re-lit. It was re-lit then, as you know, with a battery affair: turn the handle just like a cigarette-lighter: a flint and then you'd light the wick of the lamp. It was done in a *man-hole* on the side of the road. The fireman would test your lamp as you went in the morning, at the same place.

'Of course you had little incidents. I'll give you an instance when I was on the coal-cutter. A chap worked with me, and I was in charge of the coal-cutter at this particular time. We were cutting through the face of coal, and it was drawing towards meal-time. We had a matter of twelve yards to go before finishing cut the face. And I said to this fellow:

"Tom," I said, "I think we'd better go and have a bit of food."

"No, let's carry on."

"No!" I said, "let's go and have a bit of food."

'We went over the conveyor troughs to have our sandwiches; and as we got over there was a fall—right down on top of the cutting-machine. Now something told me we'd better go and have a bit of food. If we'd ha' stopped and carried on we would have both been buried. You develop that! You get that bit of instinct in you.

'Later on, I had a chance through a brother-in-law of mine to go and work in the power-station over there at Aberaman. And I came out from there and I haven't been down the colliery since. And I can tell you this: they deserve all they can get for going down there. To be honest with you, if they offered me £100 a week to go back down, I wouldn't! That's my opinion of it. If they offered me a £100 a week and I was fit, I wouldn't go. I'm suffering from pneumoconiosis from that experience—from the coal-cutters chiefly. When you were cutting the coal at that time, the dust was terrific. You couldn't see your hand in front of you. There's a different system today: water and more ventilation—but I can't say what it is.'

I met Jack Evans at the home of Mrs Gwen Netherway. Their fathers had been work-mates in the Dyffryn colliery, Mountain Ash. Her short account of her father and brother touches on one of the human aspects of mining:

"Yes, both our fathers worked together: they were work-mates; and my father had an accident on the day Mr Evans's father was not at work. Yes, his accident was in August 1914. It was due to a fall of coal. He was then taken to hospital, and after being there for three months, he came home; and my mother nursed him. He was thirty-eight when he had the accident, but he lived to be seventy-four, in spite of his disability. It was a very serious accident. He had a fractured dislocation; and it meant that the spinal cord was penetrated: he was paralysed from the waist down from then on, unable to walk at all. He had his bed here in this room, and he sat there. He used to dress himself in spite of the fact that he couldn't walk. He used to stay in his bed and dress, and then take himself round the furniture to sit in his chair every day. He was very interested in current affairs; and listened avidly to the radio; and read the newspapers. He was interested in music. He used to transpose music for me, from a lower key to a higher key if I needed it. He did all sorts of things for me: copied out songs and so on. So in spite of the fact that he was incapacitated, he didn't allow himself to vegetate at all.

'We are all of the opinion that my brother, Meurig Williams, became a spinal specialist because of my father's accident. He was only six when my father was injured; and when he was a little boy he made some wooden supports so that my father could walk backwards on his hands [dragging his legs and feet] so that he wouldn't have to bend too much. My brother made these very rough wooden supports; and I have always felt that his interest in spines dated from that time. Some years ago he invented some metal supports for insertion into the spine; and he has used these metal supports many times in operations on miners. And many of them are very grateful to him for the way these supports have helped them. Zimmers of Bridgend make those supports, and they are now called *The Meurig Williams* plates. Although he has now retired he continues to be interested in miners, and is very partial to them—always.'

In order to find out what were the effects of mechanization in a different area, where a different variety of coal was mined, I visited the Dulais valley in north Glamorgan—Seven Sisters, Onllwyn and Banwen—the rim of the coal-basin, where the coal emerges near the surface. This fact alone made the collieries here very different from the steam-coal pits I had slight acquaintance with farther south in mid-Glamorgan where the coal-basin dips to its lowest point. Many of these mines were well over 2,000 feet below the surface; but the Dulais valley collieries were chiefly drifts, tunnels that were cut from the surface and which followed the

19 Ynyscedwyn Colliery, the Dulais Valley, Glamorgan, 1906. Note the different types of headgear—from billy-cock to what appears to be a boy's stalking-cap with earpieces. Note the young boy [*centre front*] with his tommy-box and water-jack. The colliery was a drift mine, but the winding gear shows that a pit had originally been sunk here. This was later used as a ventilator shaft

BRYNTEG - 1913

20 Brynteg Colliery, Dulais Valley, 1913. By this time nearly all the men and boys have the curling-box type of cap. Note the pit-pony and the whippet. Next to the man with a drinking jack [*front*] is a man holding an unusual type of lamp, a *dart*. A spike, which allowed the lamp to be fixed to a post, was also used as a handle. The young collier on the extreme right is holding a powder-tin. Behind him is a fireman or overman; he holds the essential tools of

seam of coal down an incline, then opened out into cross tunnels or *levels* where further roadways and stalls were formed. Here the coal is very near the surface; but the steam-coal could only be reached by sinking a deep pit that might take a year or more in the making before the process of opening up and raising coal was begun. The other main difference is that the seams of coal in the steam-coal[1] districts are usually thicker, four or five feet or even more; while in the anthracite districts the seams are not only thinner but the coal itself is disposed in the earth in a different manner. Instead of being a more or less continuous layer the coal is in segments. As one of my informants told me:

'The seam of anthracite coal is divided into *slips*: the coal is leaning in *leafs*, varying from three or four inches to a yard thick; and they are slanted in a certain direction.'

The difference in the depth and the disposition of the coal-seams in these two coal-fields—the anthracite, or hard coal, and the steam, or softer coal—are emphasized here because they are claimed to have an effect both on the character of the working and of the social organization of the different mining communities associated with the particular coal-field. But it would be best for the informants to speak for themselves. Before we have their evidence, however, it is worth noting that their accounts again illustrate how a collector can approach a series of interviews. He can do so in at least two ways: he can be rigidly exclusive, keeping to one main theme, perhaps with a list of questions drafted before he starts, or he can adopt an open-ended approach where he allows his informants to be, within limits, discursive; where he gets his information incidentally, as it were, while recording the whole context of the work—by direct description, anecdote, individual evaluation and so on—with the aim of getting atmosphere and depth for the whole account. I chose the latter method; and spent some time in the anthracite area where, it appears, mechanization came rather later than in the bigger steam-coal collieries. Mining, that is, remained a craft until the early part of the last war, with each collier taking a boy as a kind of 'apprentice' into his stall; and in some instances trying him out later with another

---

[1] So called because it was the best coal for burning in steam-engines. It was the coal used by the Royal Navy before ships became oil-fired. Hence the frequency of such names as *Ocean*, *Maritime*, and *Navigation* for pits or coal-companies in south Wales.

boy, both under supervision in an adjacent stall, until they could prove themselves to be master-craftsmen, able to work the stall and be trusted to look after themselves. But sometimes before going underground a boy, on leaving school, went to work on the *screens* which were on the surface—*top-pit*. Here the coal that was brought up from underground was tipped on to a slow-moving endless belt: the boys, standing alongside, took off the slag or rubbish that was mixed with the coal. After *screening* for some months on the surface of the mine, a boy would then link up with a collier who would take him as help-mate or *butty* in his stall. Often a boy's father was the first to take him below. Hywel Jeffreys (Jeff Camnant), born 1913, described his first day underground:

'I started work at Christmas-time in Banwen colliery, the 29th of December. It was a Saturday. I had to go to sign on; and I had to show my birth certificate. After I signed, the manager told me that I'd remember that date for the rest of my life. So far he hasn't been wrong! And I was walking down with my *yorks* [straps below the knee] and my belt, everything tied and dressed properly like a collier. After we went down about a hundred yards, we had to take a spell for me to get used to the darkness underground because the small flame of the oil-lamp wasn't showing enough light. Five or ten minutes by there, and getting introduced to all the old colliers that were in the same *manhole*, that we called it: I started down then to follow my father; and I had to follow him like a little dog, all the way. And it was rough going, and I had to watch my head and I had to watch where I was putting my feet. Down a steep *hard-heading*, that is a part of the drift driven from one seam to another through a *fault*. And I went down a few hundred yards again. Then we met the firemen that were coming back to meet us—the firemen of the district where I was supposed to work. They were glad to see me and they shook me by the hand and one of them said:

"*Mae dy hâf bach di wedi passo! Mae'n rhaid iti weithio nawr.*" [Your summer is over; and now you must go to work.]

'As it was Saturday, I was only shown the place. I didn't think much of it. It was an awful long day. And the other boys were trying to talk to me, but my father wouldn't let them. An old man working in the next heading had come over in the dark and tried to frighten me. That didn't matter: I'd heard him coming. But the place was—I was surprised that the coal was shining, even with the dim light of the lamp. I couldn't make that out! It was reflecting all the time: it was anthracite coal, of course. We were making a heading going up hill. And there was gas in the heading. We couldn't raise the lamp to the roof, or the flame would rise, and it would blacken the glass—go out, you see. As there was gas we had to *work* the coal: we couldn't *fire* [use explosives] there; and we had to crop the *top*, the rock above the seam of coal, with a mandril. (We were supposed to butt out to some old level, to drain the water from another district.) It ceased to be a visit after the first day; and I was sick every night as I was coming out into the fresh air. And that's how I started! It didn't happen the first day; but in the following weeks I used to get sick from the gas; and I was doing more work and exhausting myself.

'About twelve years ago I visited my teacher in Craig-y-nos hospital; and he saw me before I saw him and he shouted "Hywel!" Nobody calls me Hywel: they always call me Jeff. I stared round; couldn't see anybody. *"Shwmae, bychan?"* [How are you, boy?] It was Wat Bach! Watkins the teacher. And I went to talk to him about school. I'd only been—I wasn't a bad scholar in school. But when I talked to him about it, the chances we'd lost; and how we could have done this and that! he said:

"Good job you had to go underground, or else you'd have been hung before now!"

'And all our class were—well, the mine was like a funnel: boys were leaving school and down the pit they had to go, swallowing them up!'

Hugh Hughes started in the mines about the same time as Hywel Jeffreys:

'I went to the mines shortly after I left school. I had to wait about three months for the job. Things were full up, and no jobs going; and I went out on the side of the road there every day to talk to John Samuel—he was the under-manager. It took three months: January, February, March, '29. I remember the first day I was down. I was so small, you see, I couldn't hold my lamp —the Davey lamp—like that. It would hit the floor! The collier gave me a shovel straight away; and I started throwing coal back; and I had to throw it back to the dram. On the first day I filled at least four tons of coal. No sentiment at all. You worked together on the face. In your stall you had fourteen yards. You had seven

1 At the coal face – this is the view a collier-boy had
   of the top of the road

yards on the upper side, three yards on top of the road, and four
yards the lower side. You had seven yards on the upper side because most places were on a gradient and it was easier to throw
down. You had to throw that coal; and it was hard work. It
was working out about a ton of coal for about a cubic yard. And
if you had fourteen yards of stall, it meant you had fourteen tons
of coal; and then you'd have a yard of *rippings* [rock ripped
down from above the seam of coal]; you'd have to bore and blow
down this from the top to make your roadway, to get your road
on.'

Evan Davies went underground when he was fifteen, in the
early 'twenties:

'But I started work on top of the colliery when I was thirteen
years of age: we were a big family, you know: ten boys and one
sister. We were all children then. So I decided now, well, I'm
going to work, anyhow, to try and help. So I went to the *screen* to
work. But I pestered my father now, and I said:

"Well, I'm going to work with my brother!"

'My oldest brother who is dead now. So I went underground
with him. It was in the winter and we started at 7 o'clock and we
weren't coming out till 4.30 in the afternoon. We never seen daylight. We were all ten boys in the family and we were all miners.

132

My father was an overman in Abercrave colliery and he was working nights. (I was only five years of age then.) And a knock came at the door; so I went to open the door now; and there was a man standing there now; a man there, said my father had an accident. So I shouted to my mother upstairs; and she came down and he said he'd had his leg off, high up. A stone came down and cut his leg off. During the time I worked with my brother we called them *pans*: iron-ore in a little flat pancake sort of thing; very heavy and very loose. If you hit the surface of the top with a mandril, it was like a bell. And then it could come down like that! One came down and broke my brother's arm. He packed up the colliery after that; became a policeman in Swansea.'

John Williams, born 1903, at Cwmtwrch in the Swansea valley, recalls an earlier period than the others:

'I started in mining in January 1918, working then with my father as was customary at the time. Each boy when he was going to the colliery would be working with his father in stall-work. And there were so many of us—there was one disadvantage of working with your father: he was not giving you any pocket money out of the pay. So we started scheming very young indeed: we schemed to go for a spell with somebody else's father—changing, you see. We might come off with about a threepenny-bit pocket money at the end of the week. But anyway, we started at 2s 7d a day; and we were having the 2s 7d and nothing more. But if you were working with a stranger—that had no children, especially—you'd be having ninepence or a shilling. This was in the anthracite district, in a colliery owned by D. W. Davies. He had three collieries, with a total of about 1,500 men. This was in the Swansea valley.

'But as for my feelings when I started work: naturally, for months before starting I used to go down and look at this slant or drift—down this drift, not only me but other boys due to start at this time; and we were looking forward to the day we would be coming down. And we'd be wearing moleskin[1] trousers about a month before starting work—except for going to school, of course. And there were things that, personally, surprised me. I was disappointed in some things: I was pleased with other things. But it was the way of living—all Sunday school, chapel, and the

---

[1] Here, the cloth: a soft, but very strong, cotton fustian.

day-school, of course. And my father happened to be a public man, a councillor, and secretary of the chapel, and things like that. And in those days, men like that used to do a lot of work for people: letters, forms, and so on. And I thought that my father was the top-dog. And living in the same village were men we called *officials*, firemen [or deputies] in the colliery. And I remember some of them used to come to my father: "What do you think of this, Joe?" or, "What do you think of that?" And I didn't think much of them: I must be candid. You see, my father was at the top! Well, my first day at work a man—Walters, one of these men I am talking about, an official—came into the stall; and my father told me now:

"Remember now, John: he's our boss."

'Well, he hit me for six! To think that that man was my father's boss! Those were the little things that disappointed me. But I looked forward to going down the mine. Yes; and that's what it was: a badge of manhood; because you sensed *that* before you went into the mine, because you were wearing the moleskin trousers. It couldn't come quick enough! I went, as I said, on 8 January, 1918, me and two other chaps (the two have gone now, passed on now), starting the same day. *Having our lamps*, they used to call it. "You're having your lamp on 8 January." The old Davey safety lamp. As I said, I was surprised with some things and disappointed with others. People were working very hard— harder than what I thought; and I wanted to learn the way to negotiate a bit too soon to suit my father, you see. He used to tell me:

"You mind your business. Do your work!"

'I used to ask him:

"What are you having for this? And what are you having for that?" And he gave me a copy of the price list.'

Before we are able to comment on the changes that took place in the anthracite areas it is necessary to get a fair idea of the physical working conditions, the layout of the colliery before mechanization. George Evans (born 1925) of Banwen gives a clear description of one of the drifts he worked in as a boy just after he started mining; and from his account and the ones that follow it is possible to visualize the physical shape of an anthracite drift-mine under the stall-system of working:

'There was a draw-out [redundancy] at the Banwen colliery,

and we went to work at the *Rhâs*.[1] The reason was France had
fallen, and we didn't have enough demand for Banwen coal.
There were about 300 men drawn out at the time. That was at the
end of 1940. So we went along to the Rhâs—about four of us. It
wasn't a colliery as we understood a colliery to be, it was just a
drift that had been driven down by a contractor, Phil Jones—
Phil y Pant we used to call him. We were sent there as boys in a
kind of utility capacity. We used to work with the colliers, do
whatever was necessary until what they called the *opening out*.[2]
Once they drive the drift down far enough, they make a *double-
parting* or marshalling yard for the drams; and then they start
branching out, making *levels*.[3] Then we were allocated to colliers
to work as collier-boys. It was a two-foot-ten seam; and the
method they used there was: they'd have a main drift going down,
following the seam of coal, and a companion following that. And
they'd drive two levels off. You'd have a main level and a companion level so that the air would percolate from one to the other.
This was the main reason. And once these levels went on far
enough, a *heading*, or main roadway, would be driven up from the
top level. And that would be a heading going back in the same
direction as the main drift was coming down. And off the heading
you'd have stalls driven off. I worked in the *level*[4] with this collier:
at first he'd drive the level along; and the manager would come
along and he'd say:

"Put forming *cogs* in, forming timber. We're going to drive a
heading."

'And we'd drive the heading, and the heading would carry on.
And another collier would be allocated the heading. Then he'd
drive the heading up; and as we'd be travelling up, he'd be making
stalls; and other colliers would come in and go into the stalls. The

[1] English *race*. There is a tradition that about 150 years ago it was the
practice to dam the mountain stream just above where this drift-mine
was opened. The water was then released: it burst from the dam and
scoured off the top soil, laying bare the iron ore that was just under the
surface. This was then carted away by pack mules.
[2] See Figs. 3, p. 138 and 4, p. 162.
[3] See Fig. 4, p. 162.
[4] 'The level is supposed to go on a *level-strike*. (They don't follow the
seams; the seams are nearly always tilted.) That's how the levels are supposed to be: to make it easier for the horses to pull out the coal.' Hywel
Jeffreys.

2 Entrance to a drift mine – opening a drift

heading was a roadway wide enough for a dram and horse to go along. And this way, you took out a block of coal complete, and had the air percolating. It was a method of ventilation: the air went up the heading and down the faces of the stalls and on to the level.'

It is interesting to speculate why the work of the miner, like the work of the farm-hand, was always considered by the generality of people to be unskilled work; and it must be admitted that the lowness of the wages in both occupations seemed to agree with this judgement: 'Why, you just went down the mine and simply dug the coal out. The skill was with the surveyors and the officials. The miner dug the coal out. Hard work, but scarcely skilled work!' Such seemed to be the general verdict; rarely stated but often implied, especially where wages were being discussed. But both mine- and farm-work were extremely skilled crafts as most people would now agree. The miner, in addition to the skills needed to win the actual coal—*reading* how the coal lay, knowing the best method to tackle a seam, handling the tools, acquiring the *instinct* that told him in his work what was the best course to follow and, in danger, how to get out—had under the old stall-system to learn the skill of handling and dressing timber. George Evans recalls this:

'I went first with a collier called Harry Thornton. I remember Harry Thornton well because I couldn't notch timber properly, and I couldn't get the top of the arms square. I remember Harry saying to me one day—there I was struggling to cut this timber—and he said to me:

"What hand do you play cricket with, George?"

'And I said: "My left hand."

"All right," he said. "Well, we'll turn this stick round, and you change the axe round and use it like a cricket bat."

'It didn't bother me afterwards. I kept it square after that. I was cutting with my wrong hand. I was trying to use it—he was right-handed, and I was following him! But I'd been a bit of—it took me six or seven months before I could do it. I was struggling: I couldn't manage it at all; when I was cutting my timber, there was a sort of bellying in the top of it because I was turning the axe upwards. I wasn't driving down the way I would with my natural swing.

'To get those great timber beams dead square—to sit, they had to be square. And oddly enough, I think that most boys found that was one of the biggest worries of all. If you worked with a nasty man—and remember, you were not like boys of today which you think of as eighteen, but boys of fourteen; and the difference between a boy of fourteen and a big collier of twenty-six was much greater than with a boy of eighteen. He'd cut the first side of the beam or the collar; he'd cut the notch. Then he'd go up to the other end, and he'd tell you:

"Right. Square that end!"

'And to get this, you didn't have no level, no set-square: you had to do this by hand and eye, by judgement. And he'd be standing there, with his big foot on the other end and his axe in his hand:

"Come on! Have you squared it? Come on! Come on!"

'If there was a mistake, you'd be in the wrong always. And he wouldn't come and help you and check. He'd say: "Is it square?"

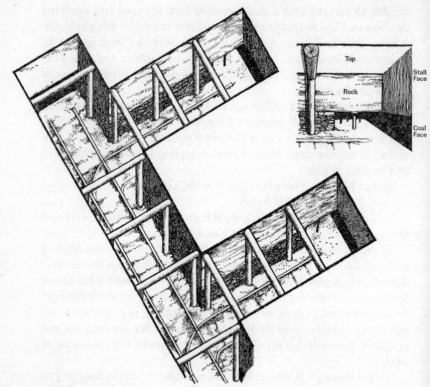

3 Colliers' stalls

and he'd just stay where he was, and he'd spit! Most of them could spit, dead on the mark. Then he'd go and notch the timber; and when you'd go and lift that timber, if it wasn't square it was your fault. It was a great worry; because it was a lot of work. He'd go and fetch his friends to help him with the collar [the 'tie-beam' joining the two 'arms' or uprights]; and when he got it up and the collar would start to rock, he'd say:

"You should have squared it!"

'The only time you used the *measuring stick*[1] was between the faces of the two arms, to get the length. But it was the boy's business to see that it was squared. You could get it square on one side, but it had to sit on the other side as well. If it didn't, as soon as the pressure of the roof came on it would just roll off.'

[1] This was usually made of wood with leather *guides*.

138

John Williams confirmed the need for skill in the timbering, and also in working the *face* of coal:

'Oh yes! Oh, you were taught. In the timbering the craft was; and working then on the face. The seam is layered on a slope, with about ten to twelve inches between the *slips*. Now you'd go into the corner now [of the stall] about five yards and work in, advance in. When you were working in that direction, digging under, you were putting in what they call a *sprag* [a short wooden support] to hold that while you were doing it. Then you knocked out all the sprags and the whole of the coal would fall. Now you had to be taught those things. A stranger coming in, however scientific he was, he'd have to be taught that, however intelligent he was. You were trained to understand the layering of the coal, to know where to look for it, and how to go at it when you find it. And another thing: you were encouraged to do it, to save explosives. Now you had to pay for explosives, at a shilling a pound. A shilling was a lot of money then, perhaps one-twelfth of your day's wage. So instead of paying for the powder, you worked a bit harder and more craftily in order to save paying for explosives. You'd often hear the term: "Now I'll do it this way, save putting powder in." And it wasn't enough to have a pick and shovel; you had to know how to use them. Even in using a shovel, you got to learn. It's not simply just lifting it up. No! We as boys, you know, handling the *top*, bringing the *rippings* down, hard stone. Well now, if you didn't know how to shovel, you'd kill yourself in about five minutes. So you were taught now: "You just take what's on the shovel until you work yourself right under." It wasn't enough, as I said, to have a pick and a shovel. People had to know how to use 'em. The same with lifting things in a small space. If you were chosen to work a *heading*—a heading is the main drive where the stalls are going off—you were a skilled man. Of course, you were the king-pin! You were chosen because you could keep the road straight—for which you were paid sixpence a yard—a big thing at that time—for keeping the road straight, sixpence a yard.'

The tools that the miners used were few and simple. They changed very little in the period before the machines came in. John Williams described first of all, an old implement that has been obsolete for half a century:

'When I started there was no machinery at all; and we had to haul the coal in the face by what we called *curling-boxes*, instead of shovels; so that you could see what you were putting in the dram, to see that you were putting no rubbish in. The curling-boxes went out just after the 1926 Strike. They weren't keen on them after that. I don't know why. But that's about the time they went out; because then price lists were moving a bit: there were changes generally in price lists throughout the south Wales coalfield.'

The curling-box was like a big metal shovel [Plate 18]. It was lifted by inserting the hands in two slots cut in the highest part of the box. In shape, the curling-box was very much like the flat cloth-caps that the majority of men wore after the First World War. The headmaster of the county school I attended in the 'twenties had noticed this similarity; and one morning, to some of the fifth and sixth form members who were getting sheepish about wearing their small school caps, he issued this injunction:

'Don't let me see any of you boys wearing those old curling-boxes in the town, or anywhere else for that matter. You have to set an example!'

George Evans used all the tools except the curling-box when he worked in a drift during the early part of the last war. The most complicated tool was the hand-drill that was used for boring holes into the *top*, the rock above the coal, into which a charge of powder was placed in order to blast the rock loose. This could only be done in those places which were free of gas:

'Well, we had to know how to put up *top-machines*, a hand-machine for drilling into the rock. [Plate 17.] Rigging a top-machine could be an ordeal if it was in an awkward place. You had to make a platform so that you could bore into the rock. And sometimes you had a crumbly roof, and you couldn't tighten the machine; because the machine, once it was boring, was under terrific pressure. The drill was trying to bite into the rock, and the only purchase the drill had was the push against the machine that you had stood. In a wet place like the Rhâs it was always a bit of a problem to get a top-machine to stand upright. Some of the men had post-machines; some had big stands. You put a post up and tightened the machine against the post. That machine for boring was worked by hand. It had two ratchet-handles on it, so the boy normally—because he was shorter than the man—would sit in the dram and work the bottom ratchet; and the man would work the ratchet at the top. He'd take the one where he was, standing out of the dram. It would take, to bore a top-hole, it would take you hours: the drill only made half a turn all the time. But when I was a boy, there were boys working in the *Brass* vein in the Onllwyn, they were still *tarading*.[1] (I've never done it myself.) That was boring with a chisel. And that was still being done in 1940 in Onllwyn colliery, in Onllwyn Number One.

'For his tools the collier would have a top-machine for boring in the rock; he'd also have a coal-boring machine or set: that is, a breast-plate, a thing that you held in front of your stomach or your chest; and it had a handle like the handle of a brace-and-bit, with a point on it. And it had a square spanner-end on it that fitted into the end of the coal-drill. The coal-drill was made of a much lighter steel than the top-drill; and you used that normally on your knees. You'd cut a notch in the rock at the bottom of the seam, and you'd put the breast-plate into it; and you had to lean against the breast-plate. If you weren't used to using it, for a boy for example, it was a painful process, because your hand used to skim against the rock at the bottom and take skin off your knuckles; or if you slipped and the breast-plate came up! Until you had the knack of it, it could be quite a painful affair. (By the way, this machine was also called *the bow-and-stand*.) You'd work until the rock would put a kind of plastic layer on you—where the skin had been taken off. And it would get stiff like as if you'd baked it in clay—till you put it into the bath in the night; and it would then start to burn.

'Then you had the mandrils—two mandrils normally. You'd have a coal-mandril which was very light and very sharp with a long—the blade was more like a stiletto; then you had a top-mandril. That was for cutting back in the rock for to put in timber arms; and this was a much more sturdy affair. You had a shovel, of course; and then you had an axe, a seven-pound axe which was kept like a lance; because the timber-work was quite extraordinary. It was as good as a carpenter's.

'The tools were kept on a bar. Each tool had a hole through it; and this bar would pass through the hole; and at the end of this bar there was a slit, a cotterell—I think they called it a cotterell—that would hold a padlock; and that was your job. The boy, when he went to work with a collier, he'd have two keys, and he'd give

---

[1] A Welsh word, partly anglicized: *taradr* = an auger, also a cold chisel in the Dulais valley; *Taradr-y-coed* = a woodpecker.

you one. You had to guard that with your life. If you lost that key! You'd get a bootlace and tie it into your waistcoat pocket like a man [with a watch]. Then you'd unlock the tools in the morning, and take off what tools you needed: shovel for you, shovel for him, two mandrils, sledge-hammer. You'd leave the timber-tools on: you'd only take those off when you needed them; coal-drills and so on. Then you'd socialize a bit with the men who were working close by, saying, "Good morning. Have you been to chapel?" and so on. Then you'd have to carry all the tools up to the face ready. And in the end of the day, he'd just say:

"Right. All right! Put the tools on the bar."

'That was the fastest job of the day! But you had to put them on tidy. Most of them would look at the iron-bar to see they were all on properly. Then perhaps he'd tell you: "Don't put the coal-drill on. Take it down to the blacksmith." So you'd take the drill out then. If the axe needed to go out to be put on the big grind-stone outside, he'd take that himself. They wouldn't give it to a boy: it would be too dangerous to carry in the dark. But any other tool—mandril or drill—the boy would take it out, and take it to the blacksmith, and tell him that Dai Williams, or whatever his name was, wanted it sharpened by the morning. And then you'd be at work in the morning, you'd collect that. None of their tools were marked. They knew their own tools by handling them.'

9

Anecdote and Atmosphere

————————————— ✳ —————————————

The importance of anecdote—plain gossip, the less kindly disposed would call it—in getting at the attitudes of people and the atmosphere in which they lived has been stressed earlier. Therefore, before going on further to describe the work conditions in an anthracite colliery and the changes in the work itself, I have collected some of the anecdotes related to me by the men I met. They help to reveal the atmosphere of the community, and also to illumine a little of the colliery background. The anecdote, that is, is an aspect of oral information that should be as scrupulously recorded by the collector of oral sources as the seemingly more weighty historical facts. Weighty facts often have a tendency to decrease in importance as time goes on, while the minuscule sometimes grows to a new dimension.

John Williams describes some of the happenings of the early 'twenties when the go-slow movement started as a form of industrial protest:

'But there was a lot of humour about, dry humour. I never heard any dirty jokes in the colliery. The chapel influence, I suppose. And you had to behave with your father. Then have you heard of *ca' canny*? I remember now us boys sitting down on a Monday morning, and another collier come on to us and sat between me and another boy; and he said:

"Now look! There's ca' canny on this morning!"

"What is ca' canny?"

"Oh, go slow."

'It appears that it was a Scotch term *call canny*—to be cute. What was happening was that the boys were working, doing all the work; and the men sitting back, discussing their tactics. So the men weren't working much, but we were just earning enough to get what they called the *cosb*[1]—the minimum wage. If you

[1] The Welsh word for *punishment*.

143

earned more than that you had to pay it back into the pool. And—personal again!—I remember going home one day; and there was a load of coal out on the road for us. It was the practice then, the women would carry in the load while the men were in the colliery. But anyway, when I got home there was a load of coal out; and my mother said:

"Now come on, John *bach*; let's get the coal in before your father comes home."

'My father, as chairman of the Lodge, was coming home later.

"Come on now! Let's get this load of coal in before he comes home. Your father's working hard. He'll be tired!"

'I told her: "Working hard!" I said, "he's been sitting on his backside all day!"

"What's the matter with you?" she said. "You shouldn't tell tales about your father!" '

George Evans relates a tale which also describes, incidentally, an aspect of the work:

'Mind you there was a lot of fun to be got in the colliery as well as hard work. Especially with Owen from Seven [Sisters]. Well, he was a collier and he was much older than me. He had had his place [his own stall]. It was snowing—and I remember it was snowing heavily; and when the dram came down it was still half full of snow, starting to melt. And Owen was boring on top of the road, stripped to the waist; and he was sweating like anything (he'd been drinking the night before). I gathered this snow: it was starting to melt so it stayed together—a big huge slab of it. He couldn't hear me; he was boring—and there was his back by there, streaming with sweat and I just laid on top of him like that and held him to the snow. I could feel his heart stopping. Dear, dear! He couldn't speak for a long time. It took his breath right away. But there was some terrible tricks underground. Handel Williams, he was a rider on a *journey*[1] of drams. They had riders then: they don't have them—they're not allowed now. It was a very dangerous job, riding was. And we had a *main-and-tail* on the journey because a level—well, it didn't go on the level: it had hills and dales in it. So we had to have a rope at both ends of the journey. Well, we'd wait for Handel to knock off the tail-rope, and then he'd go out with the journey. Then we'd catch hold of

[1] A train of trams or tubs linked together, for hauling to the surface by a steel rope.

144

the tail-rope and carry it all the way to the top of the hill and hide it. And Handel—only oil, hand-lamps we'd have then—and Handel would come back down in about half an hour's time, and there he'd be looking for the tail-rope. He was a pleasant character too, was Handel.'

Hywel Jeffreys who was with his friend Evan Davies at the time, told the kind of story that harks back to an early generation of miners whose fathers must have been among the first colliers in this area.

'The countrymen, early on, used to come in taking jobs as *repairers*.[1] The queer thing about it was, they weren't lasting very long: they were having pneumoconiosis and silicosis quicker than us. Whether we had been brought up to it and were not breathing when the dust was coming up, I don't know. Because they had local boys working with them, and those boys were lasting; and the boys were doing most of the graft, filling the muck. The old countryman would be coming in, taking a lot of pride in notching his timber, and having the right size, and all the architecture of a good repairer. But it was the labourer who was doing the heavier work, and he was poorer paid.—But I got to tell you one story: somehow or other, when I was in my forties I worked by an old man who was sixty-six. I had to work afternoons because of trouble in the house there: it was illness. But this old man preferred to work on the afternoon shift, to save getting up in the morning. All he wanted was a drink on the way home from work. That's all he wanted was his little pint. But his stories were superb. He was born and lived in a farm about three and a half miles from the colliery. But his father and his brothers were working in the colliery: he was the youngest son. And there was a method at that time when a boy had to do so many years as a *door-boy* for the *halliers*;[2] and that wasn't good money. But when he come stronger he was allowed to go with a collier. So the father wanted one of his sons who had been door-boy to finish and to come and work with him; because he was old enough; he'd been on it for so long. Telling the manager this now; and the manager said:

[1] Timber repairer: his job was to maintain the roadways or tunnels.
[2] The boy had to open the brattice doors for the hauliers to take the pony and dram through. The doors were kept closed to regulate the ventilation. This was an extremely lonely job; and very young boys used to do this work when the mines first opened.

"You can have Joseph to work with you, if you can bring another one instead of him. Have you got another one in the house?"

"Oh, I got one in the house; but he's too small. But I'll bring him till I can get somebody instead of him!"

'So Tom that I was working with, the old man of sixty-six, had to start work at ten and a half years of age as a door-boy until they had somebody instead of him. Well, I worked with him for about five years; and we were always getting places next to each other. But eventually Tom became seventy; and I said to him as he was finishing that day:

"Well, they're sure to be having somebody instead of you now, Tom!" *'Dychi nabod e'? Tom Pugh, tad Edgar.* [H.J. to E.D. Do you know him? Tom Pugh, Edgar's father.] A jovial old man!'

Evan Davies was born in the adjoining valley and started work in one of the mines near his home:

'The colliery was owned then by private people: Davies and Morgans of Abercrave; and they weren't paying, no minimum wage, or anything like that then. I'd work a full week—well, I've known people, old men who'd work a full week there with a boy; and not have a ha'penny to pay the boy; had to borrow money on the Monday to pay the boy. So they were always short of labour there. And people from Merthyr,[1] and Spaniards, Portuguese, all coming to the colliery asking for a job.

"Yes, start today."

'I remember two or three Spaniards coming there to work. Political troubles it was. (No, it was well before the Spanish Civil War.) No money, no idea! So there was a shop there (I don't know if Jeff remembers it), Jones's shop. They'd give them a note, and they'd go down to the shop and get what they want: tools and enough food. And the first pay they had that was taken out. You had nothing at all the first week to spend.'

Hywel Jeffreys, who was being interviewed, with Evan Davies, put in:

'There were Frenchmen owned the mines: there was a French company owned two collieries where Ifan used to work in Abercrave. They used to have huts down there by the *Lamb and Flag* [pub]. Then they had a big shed by the colliery; sleeping rough there, you know.'

[1] About three-quarters of the men in this north Glamorgan borough were unemployed during the late 'twenties and most of the 'thirties.

Evan Davies went on: 'Yes, the time the Spaniards and Portuguese came to Abercrave. Yes, they all worked underground, which they didn't know nothing about, at all; and they wouldn't speak up; and there were no rights there. The manager used to tell them:

"Well, if you don't want it, you know where to go!"

'Well, I don't think there's one of them alive now. They stayed; they had houses here; they spoke Welsh; they learned Welsh here. They came during the trouble out in Spain—before the Spanish Civil War—about ten families came here.'

Hywel Jeffreys: 'Can you remember, Ifan, that French company used to have metal collars for their horses, to stop them having these *marbles* on their necks; *Warwicks* they called them. They had to get hardened to it, no doubt, but I should imagine that any old splinters and things like that would fall off the collar easier from the metal than the flannel on the inside of the ordinary horse collar.'[1]

Evan Davies: 'Horses! They were making more fuss for the horses, where we used to work, than a man. If a horse got killed— oh, big enquiry! But if a man—*psst*! just a stroke on a paper. Oh, they were bad! Starvation time in Abercrave there, with that company. I had 8s 6d as a boy on the surface: when I went underground with my brother, I had 12s 6d. I used to get sixpence pocket money on a Saturday night. We were a lot of boys, you see, my mother couldn't afford to give us. We used to go down to the fish-shop and have fish-and-chips for fourpence—then in at the shop for a pennorth of monkey-nuts. Go to the pictures [films] then, if you could find an egg to go down [to gain admission to the 'pictures']. I remember the *Sailors' and Soldiers' Week*: Egg-week we used to call it. And we'd go up to the woods above Abercrave *Welfare*. Perhaps *Dick Mock*—we used to call him then—if he'd seen a broody hen on the clutch of eggs, off she was going! and us boys an egg each and taking them down to the pictures. A rough time!

'And we used to go out on a Saturday to play football. We were eight brothers playing in the same team in Abercrave. Asking for

[1] Metal collars, made from a light aluminium-like alloy were sometimes used on East Anglian farms. If a horse was *collar-proud*, finding it difficult to wear an ordinary collar, through over-heating, the metal collar was tried. It was designed to keep the neck cool.

permission now to go out early; send the Chairman [of the Club] in to ask for permission now for Saturday, leave early to have a game. No! We had to come out and run home, and just wash our hands and face. And my mother had case and jersey and stockings and all ready. And up to the football field. After the game we used to jump into the river, and have a wash by there. I used to play full back. Well, I packed up there. Left Abercrave. I was courting and I married a girl from Colbren here, so I went to Onllwyn by here—which is closed now—and I worked thirty-nine years there—and a bit.'

John Williams, who later became manager of Banwen colliery, told of an incident that illustrates the *instinct* the miner developed:

'In stall-work underground you hardly ever heard of or saw any man hitting his head against the roof. When hard hats came in first—well, we didn't know what they wanted them for. You'd see a man walking along a road underground; and of course his sight is on the road itself. But instinctively, like a bat, he knows, *This is low*, without having to think about it. That's one of the things that you learned—came natural to you. Well, I was going down Seven Sisters pit one day: a man had come as Assistant Chief Engineer in the area. He was coming down in the same cage; and we were walking along. And do you know, he was walking inside the curve! I didn't know who he was, a stranger to me, so I told him:

"Come this side," I told him now. "You mustn't ever walk on that side!"

'And he had come in as Assistant Chief Engineer!

'You see, if there is a curve going around there, in the road, and the curve in the rope is held by rollers, and if a roller was to break, the rope that is pulling the journey comes into the short side. It could break your leg, and worse! He was not used to underground, you see.'

Before Nationalization John Williams had managed one of the collieries owned by Evans-Bevan; and as manager he used to negotiate with union officials along with the owner:

'Arthur Horner now. Arthur Horner was a chief of the Union in south Wales.[1] And we were meeting Arthur Horner one day, and Dai Dan Evans. I must say this about Arthur Horner: he was

---

[1] Later Secretary of the National Union of Mineworkers.

straight-forward; he'd stick to his line. After they had gone Bevan asked me:

"What do you think of Arthur Horner?"

"Well," I said, "he's dead straight. When he puts a case you can't very well fault him."

"I think he's a good man," he said, "a very good man!"

'There was an arrangement in the colliery: it was a silly affair altogether, the way the men were paid in a section of mechanization. One man could hang around and not do his stint; and he'd be only sixpence worse off at the end of the week than a man who had worked hard. And I didn't like it; so I made a new scheme out. And Arthur Horner said—he told the boys:

"The carrot is there for you. Take it!"

'But they wouldn't take it: they were afraid they were going to lose something. Dai Dan [Evans] and Arthur Horner—but I saw Arthur Horner, he was co-chairman in the Dispute Committee [under the National Coal Board]. By damn, the men had to put a good case to him before he—he was watching whether you were sound, every time. Funny thing, Arthur Horner used to work in a colliery up in Aberdare or Rhondda way somewhere—Maerdy, was it? And the old manager of this pit in Maerdy had another job under the N.C.B.; he went round the collieries. I think his name was Price, but it may be Rees. And he was with me in the colliery one day, and Dai Dan came on the telephone; wanted to meet me, or something like that. And Price said:

"One of Arthur Horner's friends; a Communist!"

'I said, "Yes."

"Do you know this?" he said. "That's the straightest man I ever met," he said. "Arthur Horner: you couldn't get him!"

'To get him out of the colliery without openly victimizing him, they put him to work on a stretch of drift-way; icicles hanging on it. Nobody else would work there. They put Arthur Horner to work there to keep the place clean, about 800 yards of a length, just keep it clean and things like that. They couldn't have men to do the job properly: it was too cold. So they put Arthur Horner there, thinking now:

"Oh, he'll chuck it up now!"

'But Price told me:

"No! You couldn't fault him. The place was like a bloody parlour there. And whenever you'd go down that drift, you'd see

Arthur Horner's light, right in the middle of the drift: he'd not be sleeping in the man-hole!"

'I didn't have a lot to do with Arthur Horner, but the times I did meet him he was pretty straight-forward.'

Finally, Hywel Jeffreys discussed the miners', and especially his own, attitude to accidents:

'I had a number of *hard-lines*—narrow escapes. But the queer thing about hard-lines underground is, you forget about it. If you are nearly run over by a car, you remember it for the rest of your life. It's as if we, well, expected to have narrow shaves underground. I did once; this was in stall-work; and I wasn't very old then, about twenty-three, twenty-four. And I had bored two holes, and we had rammed one and fired one. But it blew the main post on top of the road out; and I told the shotsman:

"Well, you'll have to wait now. I'll have to get this post back."

'It was a long post about eight feet, and I had a thick, long tram-line sleeper on top of it. And I told the shotsman the *top* was bad there; and if we fired the other hole before I had the post up, we might bring the whole place in. Well, I was throwing the coal away now to get at the butt where I'd stamped for the post, and I heard a scream. This big stone had fallen! It took a piece out of my flannel shirt; and I got out of it, and I brought the shovel! The stone was six feet long and over a foot deep in the thickest end, and a yard in width, coming out like a razor-edge. And I went back to see what we'd—might as well fire the hole. And the shot-firer shouted:

"Come and sit down! Come and sit down! You fool!"

"It's safe now."

"You didn't see it fall!" he told me.

'He was watching and he couldn't do nothing: he screamed. How I got out, I don't know because I was bent up. And how the piece of my father's shirt came out, caught by the stone, I don't know: coming in the same time—it ripped it as it was passing. But it didn't touch me. There was a bit of slack in my shoulders, and it took a piece out of the shirt. I went home; I didn't say anything about it; didn't think of it until my eldest brother came home:

"*G'est ti gynnig heddi!*" (You had a close shave today!) *Oedd Ifan Jones yn gweithio ag e'.* (Evan Jones was working with him [and told him.]) It came back then to my mind about the stone. I expect everybody was the same as me. Other things were cropping up, and you don't think about it, except when you are relating this, you see.

'Another time I went to the under-manager and told him:

"I think you'd better get those *partings* [cast-iron tram-rail junctions] I've recovered from the old workings back because of the open-cast. I can feel the crane bumping on top of us."

"Oh no!" said the under-manager. "I've taken care of him. I've got everything surveyed!"

'But they took the partings I had out of the old workings; and to please me he came round on the Monday:

"Oh, you're safe enough by here, Jeff. You're safe enough!"

'The following day I'd put a pair of timber up, and I'd pulled a lump, and I was supposed to knock out into some airway. And the fireman was bringing a labourer with him to knock at times [to test the sound of the wall of rock]. Oh! this fall started coming! And I could see light! And I shouted to them:

"Go back! Go back! The place is coming in! The place is coming in!"

'And I was moving back myself, and I was shouting as the light was coming more. It was daylight! There was a tremendous hole there right up to the open-cast [mine on the surface]. A couple of minutes later, a pile of rubbish that the open-cast people had placed slid into the hole and left a sort of chimney there that was holding four feet of coal on top of there. That was the end of that place. Another time—I didn't see this myself: it was on a Sunday; but a cow's legs went through the timber, poking down into the ground into the main drift. It had walked over the top of a shallow drift, and it had fallen through!'

10

The Underground Structure

————————————— ✳ —————————————

It has been implied that to understand the basic structure of the social relations in a working community we have, first and foremost, to study the work itself in some detail: in other words we have to know the material culture at least moderately well. For it is the kernel of our thesis that a man's attitude to his fellows grows, at least in part, out of the terms and conditions under which he works. Getting oral evidence from the people who actually did the work is—it is submitted—the best method of understanding both the work itself and the way it affects or conditions social organization. It is, moreover, manifestly valuable as a method of research for the reason that your informants can be questioned and are immediately able to amplify any aspect of the work or their work-relations that you do not understand. For it is the details, the small, seemingly insignificant but often complicated and important details, barely comprehended by those who are not familiar with the work, that are likely to be vital to a real appreciation of the workers' attitude to their job and their attitude towards one another.

Some of these details are revealed in the *price list* which ordered the method of payment in the collieries for work done. The price list was important because there was not a uniform rate of payment to the miners; although there was supposed to be a minimum figure below which a man's weekly wage could not fall. The rate of payment depended largely on the condition of his working-place. One man would have a good stall where the coal was easy to win; another would have to handle a large amount of *rubbish* or *muck* (rock) before he could begin to shift coal; another man might have a *wet place* and be constantly troubled by water. The first man needed no help: the others were compensated for their difficulties according to an agreed rate which was fixed in the *price list*.

The Underground Structure

The price list and the bargaining over it—perhaps *horse-trading* would be a more descriptive term—appear to be have been doubly important in the anthracite areas because here the collieries were labour-intensive rather than capital-intensive, to use the modern jargon. The anthracite mines were on the coal-outcrop, as John Williams explains; and a small entrepreneur with very little capital could start a colliery and begin to win coal almost immediately. He would then be able to pay his wage-bill from the sale of his product almost in the first week of his operation. And later as he went further in and *opened out* his colliery he would be able to accumulate capital. The owner of the colliery, therefore, was 'one of them', one of the community, in the sense that the miners could meet him face to face nearly every day. He was not remote, even though in a different sense his interests and theirs were polar opposites: he wanting to make as much profit as he could; and they seeking—indeed forced—to improve their working and living conditions. Farther south, in contrast, in mid-Glamorgan, tens of thousands, perhaps hundreds of thousands of pounds, had to be invested before the deep coal-seams could be reached. John Williams expands this in a note written after our conversation:

'The larger companies in the Rhondda and east Wales areas were directed mainly by people who were remote from the work-force. They could lay down stricter conditions of pay; and had the power to enforce them. To a large degree, they could dictate the terms on a "Take-it-or-leave-it" basis. Again, geological conditions in those areas were more stable: they were freer of geological disturbances,[1] without the sharp variations you find in the anthracite field. Moreover, in the anthracite area, colliery owners were part of the community; and you could sum it up by saying: Familiarity breeds contempt.'

These facts were bound to have a tremendous effect on the *feel* of the two coal-fields: first in the more obvious aspects—the conditions and methods of working, their scale, their tradition and so on—and then in the community itself. Briefly, it was the difference

---

[1] George Evans: 'Jeff Camnant drove the main for ages in the *Cornish* seam at Banwen colliery. It had been worked many times before, but the water and the geology had beaten them. In the end it beat everybody. One day you would be going straight up: the next, straight down; and at times you'd be up to your ears in water. I worked in the *Cornish* for three years: it was where I knocked my eye out.'

—at least at first—between small-scale capitalism and larger, more sophisticated undertakings. John Williams brings this out in the following account which also shows how oral evidence can reveal the nuances, the contrasts and complications that shelter underneath a generalization or simplification like the *south Wales coalfield*. But first of all to Hywel Jeffreys who explains the price list succinctly but forcefully:

'We were working on the price list: the thinner the coal, the more we were getting paid for it; but the thicker the coal, the less we'd get; and you also had the business of how much *muck* was falling with the coal. You had something for that, extra on the ton; ha'penny for six inches per ton. But I was brought up to work with my father and I understood the price list grand so I could compete with the fellow who was measuring. Others who were strangers didn't know as much as I did; and they [the measurers] weren't including certain items. I know for a fact that my brother that was older than me, a bigger fellow, two stones heavier, conscientious!—and me working next stall to him taking more home than him, simply because I was watching for the rip, the waste, water, overhead—all of it. I had it! All was material for my mother, just the same; and only a slice of it I'd have. But I did have that aggression: I wanted everything right; I'd never cheat; I wouldn't cheat. But what I'd done I wanted paid for!'

John Williams:

'But, do you know, the mine-owner—he was a very hard man, old Davies. Him and my father used to call each other by their Christian names. I'd heard him talk a lot about old Dafydd, the owner; and I thought Dafydd was a very kind man. But when I saw what was being done for him, and what the men were having, I was rather disappointed; and my image of David—Dafydd— passed away. I didn't like Dafydd any more.

'But there was a sense of co-operation, and you'll find it in the anthracite more than in other places. Because you didn't need a lot of capital—I'm digressing now—you didn't need a lot of capital to get an anthracite mine, a drift-mine. You were into the coal, and you were getting your capital out of the coal. And that is how old Davies worked his colliery. So there was an intimate feeling between the mine-owner and the worker. They despised each other! The result was, the miner would cheat the owner; and the owner would cheat the miner. But in between you got the officials, manager, under-manager; and they were working things quietly to make it easier for the miner. For instance, if the standard thickness of your seam was two feet six, you'd get 1s 8d a ton for working the coal. But for every inch below that you might get a ha'penny or a farthing for every inch—extra on the ton. And when the officials were coming round every week measuring [to see how much work had been done] the method was: the fireman to go and measure in three places along your stall and give the average. The manager and the under-manager would be sitting back on the road with the collier. And he'd call out:

"What's the average?"

"Oh, two foot three."

'And the seam might be two foot eight average! "Well," I thought, "here's a lot of liars; else they can't measure!" I didn't realize that it was a quiet understanding between them to get a little bit more on the ton. So I asked my father about it and he said:

"You want to know too much. You mind your business!"

'But it came to this: after a few months I'd come to know the terminology: what was this and what was that; and the *cogs*. These were forms of timber you were laying down to support the roof. My father told me:

"You must sit with me now,"—to train me to negotiate. "You must sit with me now." When the manager or the under-manager came round:

"What have you got, Joseph?"

'And the fireman would call out the average; and then: "Four and a half cogs." Damn it all! We hadn't put a cog in, mun! I couldn't understand it now; but I didn't say anything. And I went home and I told my mother my father was a liar. You know, my image of my father was broken. I said: "He's a liar. He's saying lies!" So I explained to her; and, do you know, she couldn't understand it. Oh, she couldn't understand it at all! But it was something—an understanding between the management and the men. Even the owner didn't know about it.'

John Williams went on to explain how the chapel and religion was involved with the work. Undoubtedly, the influence of the chapel in the mining areas of south Wales has been underestimated. It was, at least in the first two decades of the century, a lively debating ground; and the Sunday school and men's clubs often nourished a criticism of religious dogma that became a spring-board for social criticism and, later, direct confrontation with orthodox economic dogma. In fact, many of the miners' leaders, especially in the early period, were active chapel-members, some of them even lay-preachers who turned their gift of oratory to a nearer and more visible target—the coal-owner instead of the Devil. Naturally, there was—as in every place and at every period—a degree of social 'policy' in much of the chapel-going, as one of the more realistic miners suggested:

'When there was a religious manager who was going to a certain chapel, that chapel was full; and God help the poor bugger that was drinking. He'd have a place [underground], wouldn't he! He couldn't have half a shift off to go to his mother's funeral. But it was working the same way again, if the manager was a boozer: God help the ones that were pretending to be religious!'

But, all in all, in its heyday the chapel was a positive and saving force in the mining valleys, helping to soften some of the inevitable hardness and brutality that the conditions of work and the periodic and recurring poverty engendered.

John Williams: 'Do you know, the chapel was a big thing at the time. And my father was chairman of the *Lodge* [The trade union branch. A Lodge of the union was attached to each colliery] as well as being secretary of the chapel. I remember him telling me, years after, that they went to meet Dafydd in his house—the owner, in his house. There was a ha'penny a ton dispute over the price list. And prayer first. Asking the blessing of God now on the meeting. My father, two committee-men and the miners' agent; and old Dafydd and his manager, old Peter. And then they'd go on for hours, arguing about this ha'penny. But the ha'penny wasn't forthcoming. And, of course, when it came to a deadlock, they'd all stand up and pray again for God's guidance—or something like that. That was the fashion of those days, especially down there, anyway. But inside the colliery itself: "We can't get the ha'penny. . . ." because, the fact was, Davies the owner wouldn't be allowed to give it. He was guided by the coal-owners, his fellow coal-owners:

"Don't you give more than 1s 8d for that!"

'But inside the colliery, there was a whisper now, the manager whispering to my father, and we soon saw what was going on. (That's why I emphasized: what are *cogs*? a form of timber to support the roof.) For in the case of that ha'penny some arrangement came about:

"We'll give you a long post for every twelve tons of coal!"

'Now I'm coming back to the system of cogs [which were made from a long post]: the price of a long post was sixpence:

"So for every twelve tons you fill you'll get sixpence. And we'll call it a long post!"

'So they were having their ha'penny after all. Can you follow?'

The intricacies of the price list and the complications of the bargaining, the subterfuges and double standard of morality that were used by both sides to circumvent it, were among the chief reasons why the boys who entered the industry were kept in ignorance in their early months underground. They were not admitted to the 'long-house', the society of the men, until they had absorbed the skill of negotiating as well as the skill of the craft. They had to have sharp tools in both these skills, because in the period to which John Williams is referring there was a particularly bitter conflict between the miners and the coal-owners. For coal was then virtually the only source of power: therefore it was the base of most industries. The market-price of coal dictated the price of any manufactured commodity as much as did the cost of wages. Accordingly, the demand for cheap coal was perpetual and insistent; as insistent as the demand for cheap food. (Incidentally, it may be remarked as a glaring contradiction in a society that claimed to be just and equitable, that the two 'primary' class of producers—the coal-miners and the farm-workers—were among the lowest, if not positively the lowest, paid.) But the miners were at the centre-point of tension in the industrial society of half a century ago. Negotiation, skill in bargaining, was thus vital to them in order to avoid the too sharp edge of exploitation. They had had a long and hard training in this, and in countering the numerous kinds of manipulation that were used in an attempt to sell them an agreement that was not basically in their own interest. This is the reason why the miners have so often become a stumbling block to an unsympathetic Government. Through long experience at a tension-point of industrial society they recognize that democratic government as we know it is largely the art of manipulation; and they have had practice enough in detecting the trend that goes counter to their own welfare however astutely dressed or concealed it is.

John Williams: 'But we were kept—I and the other boys, were kept out of it for a few months until you came to learn to *work your own side :* your own side of the face; and your father would take the other side. It was then you were taught to *best* the owner and how to defend yourself against him. And that is why, that is why the anthracite was different from the big companies, P. D. [Powell Dyffryn] and the Corys, and those companies. They paid no dispute money nor no allowances or anything like that. But in the anthracite, with this intimacy between the owners and the work-men, knowing each other in public life and things like that, there was ripe, all-round cheating. There was no question about it. So when *Nationalization* came now, a lot of those things had to be explained. "Why!"—for instance, in Tirbach where I was work-ing then, and other collieries, they'd say: "Why! Look here! You haven't put any cogs in!" Well, the old people didn't understand that. [The cogs though mythical had become their prescriptive right!] So you were having these little disputes, you see. There was a dispute in Seven Sisters over a penny a ton, paid by some other means. But when the N.C.B. auditors came along:

"Oh, we'll check this. Oh! they shouldn't have had a penny!"

'That was the reason why there were so many disputes in the anthracite coal-field—there's no question about it—when Nationalization came in. Or even before when big companies were taking collieries over. There were always disputes about prices.

'But I did learn very early—as I said in that [BBC] programme, *The Big Hewer*—I learned to hit with the hammer of hate against the anvil of bitterness. I was feeling—I wouldn't say I was dif-ferent from other boys; but I was more interested. I became the leader of the boys in the *St Aldwyn's Award*.[1] The boys had to be kept in their place in the beginning. You mustn't know it all. You must get developed, and tuned into the wave-length, now, in this cheating. As I told you, my first reaction, when I heard about the cogs, was: "My father is a liar! He's saying lies. He's

[1] Under the Coal Mines (Minimum Wage) Act, 1912, a Joint Board was set up, comprising representatives of the colliery owners of south Wales and Monmouthshire, and representatives of the workmen em-ployed in the collieries. They met at Cardiff under the chairmanship of Lord St Aldwyn. The minimum wage agreed upon for boys under fifteen was 1s 6d a day, rising to 3s 0d for a boy over twenty and under twenty-one. These were raised to 2s 3d and 4s 6d respectively by 1915.

having money on false pretences." I didn't use that term then, of course: "He's a liar!"

'Peculiar to some collieries, they put two boys working together on shares for a period of a year or two, just to test them out. Then you'd have a place of your own. You were king in your own stall then! Because all these fathers and uncles and whatever they were —colliers—they *were* kings of the stall. And it was a wonderful society! Each couple would go to their stalls. First, there'd be a little rest period, all together—sitting down together. Perhaps twelve couples: the boys over here, and the men over there—fifteen or twenty yards between them. And you'd go on then—the term was *mwcin* (it's a word that comes from smoking). We'd say in Welsh: *"Dere! Cawn ni mwcin bach"* [Come on, we'll have a little spell]. Of course, there was no smoking going on. Then on to the stall; call to food again, later, a break. And they'd all come together again, marching to the one place and sit together: men together, colliers; and the boys together. And, of course, looking back what was interesting to me in those talks: you start the week, Mondays; talk would be nothing but chapel, you see: "Who was preaching with you last night? What was his text?" And as you go through the week, things were going away from the chapel. Looking forward now to what the team was going to do on Saturday—the rugby team, in each place, you see. And there was that cycle every week. Monday, Tuesday it was nothing but chapel, what happened on Sunday. And I remember an old fellow—he was a member of a club, mun, a drinking club—walking about three miles every Sunday (Old Will Whatley his name was); well, he was a cast-off in the middle of them all! He was somebody from the planets or somewhere!'

George Evans and Evan Davies confirmed the old hierarchy under the stall system. Evan Davies recalled a period in the 'twenties:

'I used to work in headings: two headings went up together, and there were stalls from one face to the other. When we was having food there, all the boys used to come down together and have a chat, for about twenty minutes, that's all. You could hear anything that was going on; you'd have it by there. If there was any gossip, by there you had it.'

George Evans talked about a later time, just before the start of mechanization:

'The first time you'd see this kind of order was in the morning when you went underground. The boy would go along, and he'd pick up the powder-tin, and he'd go to the blacksmith shop, and he'd pick up any drills that had been sharpened. And then you went underground. You had your lamp, of course, with you then; and you'd have to wait at the *locking-station*[1] then. The men congregated together and the boys congregated together: it was unheard of then for a boy to go and sit with the men. Or if—as I was telling you—if a boy even ventured an opinion in amongst the men, it was the biggest crime you could commit. And this was the order of things. When you went to the face and you were having your morning break perhaps only you and your *butty* would be together, and you'd sit with him. But if there were—if you were like I was: in a heading with a lot of boys, the boys would sit together and the men would sit together. And it stayed like that and it never altered. Walking out afterwards the boys would walk out together, and the men would walk out together. The boys never fraternized with the men: they were always kept strictly in their place. During the time that I was there I can't remember an occasion when the boys were allowed to join in with the men in anything; until he had a collier's *number*. Then he'd be a man then. And he could join in the *jaw*: he could talk with the men. He changed his status!'

One aspect of the organization underground has not been touched on directly; that is the pressure on individuals either by the management or the owners to comply with their interpretation of the order of things. The blanket term used by the men was *victimization*. It took many forms. John Williams who became a colliery manager in 1934, and later manager of the Banwen colliery under the National Coal Board, described how as a young man he had an early glimpse of one kind of *persuasion*:

[1] Before the introduction of the electric cap-lamp, each man carried a Davey-type lamp. This had a flame fed by oil, and each lamp had to be tested by a fireman at his locking-station or check-point as they came in at the start of a shift. Underground, too, there was also a lamp-station: if a man's lamp went out while he was at work, he could relight it by means of the *lighter* which was kept in the lamp-station. This machine re-ignited the wick of the lamp with an electric spark. Firemen still carried the Davey safety-lamp after cap-lamps came in. The flame in this lamp reacted in the presence of gas and indicated whether it was safe or not to work in the area.

'I was an agitator—or whatever you call it: I was leading the boys, and the younger miners after that. And an old official told me:

"I want to have a few words with you, John. Now you've passed your fireman's certificate; but a certificate is no good to you unless you got a job! And going on as you are, you won't get a job as a fireman."

"Well, what about it?"

"Well, if you went for the certificate you want the job, don't you?"

"I didn't say that!" and I hinted that my father wanted me to go into the pulpit, and there was a little clash between us.

"No!" he said, "you'll never get a job as long as your father is taking *The Daily Herald*!"

'That is a fact. That was in the 'twenties—1927. And I was told I would never get a job as a fireman. And I never did have. Never did have it!

"Because you got to learn," they said. "You've got to learn. You've got to behave."

'That was the word: you got to behave! I remember it quite well. I was working in a *hard heading*[1] at the time.

'And later I passed my under-manager's certificate, and I was never offered a job. And it happened one day that a shot-firer was missing on the following shift; and they had nobody else to turn to except me. And they asked me: "Would you fill the job for this afternoon?" I said, "All right." And it was like that for the two days. The following week I wasn't paid for the two days—the extra. An error in booking it was, or something like that. Going back now, and the acting-manager was in the office; the manager was away. I told him, and—do you know—he said:

"Don't you feel proud that you've been honoured to be a shot-firer for two days?"

'That's the things you had to fight!'

Hywel Jeffreys quoted an instance of where the management had used the price list not in a worker's favour but against him:

'I once worked across an old man who thought "to take me across him". He was in the level, and he had to take me across him. He had to have somebody across him—double-shift now—to turn this heading. And he was a religious man:

[1] A heading or tunnel cut through rock. Hard headings were usually driven on contract.

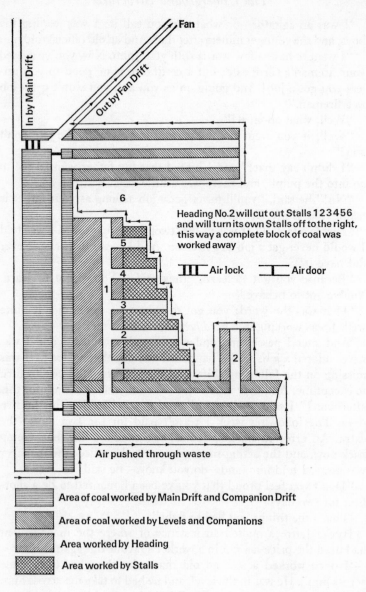

Heading No.2 will cut out Stalls 1 2 3 4 5 6 and will turn its own Stalls off to the right, this way a complete block of coal was worked away

▥▥▥ Air lock   ⊏⊐ Air door

Air pushed through waste

▥ Area of coal worked by Main Drift and Companion Drift

⟋ Area of coal worked by Levels and Companions

⟍ Area worked by Heading

▩ Area worked by Stalls

4   Plan of a drift mine to show headings driven off level to cut off stalls

"By right," he said [very deliberately], "I should have that boy to come across me. It's he who is first getting cut out."[1]

'And I was terrified to go across him. Do you know what he was doing? He was putting every stone, that was falling, on the wall: the side of his place was like a mason had been there. The road-posts were in line. And before he'd go out in the night, he was taking his cap and brushing the floor and shovelling that in the curling-box. David Lewis: that was his name. He was a very strong Labour man; and he was spouting too much and he was punished for it.

'I had to work across him. It took six weeks now to turn the heading, rip it in, and for me to have a stall ready. I stayed in that heading. But when the next heading was supposed to be turned, and they asked him who was going with him:

"Oh, this boy!"

'About me! There was no doubt about it. Now that I was "coming across" him he was happy about it. Well, about six weeks afterwards we hit a fault, and we finished. And the old man then told me:

"Jeff! I've never earned so much money in my life as when you were working across me."

'What do you think of that? But he had been rooked all his life because he was a big mouth; and he didn't know what to claim for. I knew the list, and I wouldn't let them get away with anything. It was an awful shock. And I was feeling a small man compared with him. And in his way of working, everything had to be right. And he was one mass of sweat from the beginning to the end of the shift.'

[1] See Fig. 4.

II

Mechanization

--------------------------------※--------------------------------

The coming of mechanization broke up the old hierarchy underground. It also affected the wider community for the following reason: as the miners themselves emphasized, there was a direct carry-over of status from underground to the society outside. The Lodge secretary, the check-weigher[1] and the colliery officials were usually prominent in affairs in the village; and a collier of outstanding skill like Hywel Jeffreys, who was chosen to drive *hard headings*, who was of the *Big Hewer* type celebrated in most mining areas of Britain, commanded a respect among his work-mates that gave him status in the larger community outside the colliery. There was a similar pattern in the arable areas, in East Anglia for instance, where an exceptionally skilled horseman was respected not only on the farm itself but in the surrounding district. Much of this, both in the mine and on the farm, disappeared or was greatly modified after mechanization.

But in the anthracite collieries of the Dulais valley the old underground order was challenged even before the advent of mechanization. The movement came from the boys. As John Williams has implied, and as George Evans states more specifically below, the boys themselves began to chafe at the restrictions of the stall-system as it had traditionally developed. George Evans suggests that change in the later 'thirties had an immediate effect: this was the time when the level of unemployment, especially in the mining areas, had forced the Government to set up schemes for retraining in alternative skills. Many young boys had gone out of the mining areas, and had compared their position with that of boys elsewhere. When they returned they saw the old system in a different light, and were ready to challenge it. George Evans

[1] He was the official, chosen by the miners through their trade union lodge, to guard their interests by checking the weight of each tram of coal immediately it was wound up from underground.

touches on the boys' main grievances; and he later explains how the whole work-structure, particularly as it affected the boys, altered under mechanization:

'As a boy you could work with wonderful people like Taliessin Williams. Taliessin Williams, he used to give me pocket money even after I joined the army. Him and Harry Thornton used to give me six shillings each every week. They were exceptionally good colliers who'd look after you as good as your father would look after you. But some of the boys who worked for bad colliers, they'd have to wait for their pay. The pay was included in the collier's packet, and the boy had to wait for the collier to hand him the money. And sometimes you'd work on a Saturday—it was a six-day week then—you'd go in; but your butty, the collier, wouldn't be in. And say you were a boy of seventeen, becoming competent, they'd put you to work between two colliers in a stall. But you'd have to mark your coal up on your collier's number;[1] and the chap was still in bed! But you'd have to mark the coal on him. But if he was a decent chap—which most of them were—they'd just give you the money. But some wouldn't! They saw it as a day's profit. Capitalism isn't confined to the stock-market, you see!

'The boy would have, perhaps, to go down to the collier's, his butty's, house; and perhaps his wife would say: "He's gone out!" Then perhaps the boy would see the butty on Monday; and if the butty was a bit of a spendthrift, instead of twenty-eight shillings he'd get perhaps twenty-five; and the boy would have to wait till the following week.

'This was one of the reasons, plus the whole status of boys, which caused what they called *The Boys' Dispute* in the Dulais valley in the 1940s. It was—they were quite separate incidents though lots of people thought they were an organized thing. At the time, what made people think it was organized was because the Y.C.L. [Young Communists' League] began to flourish up here; and people began to think that one went with the other. Well, I believe that one of the people involved with the Seven Sisters *Boys' Dispute* was Shôb Nicholas; and he was quite prominent in the Y.C.L.; and I was a member of the Y.C.L.; and I was in-

---

[1] It was the boy's job to chalk the collier's number on each side of the tram as it was filled with coal; and it would then be credited to the collier when it was check-weighed on the surface of the mine.

volved in it in the Rhâs colliery. But they were quite separate things really. One of the first things that sparked it off in the Rhâs was the water. You worked in terrible water in the Rhâs. And the people who had to come out in January—fill drams of coal underground, you know, and come out. You know how the wind can blow on the top in Banwen.[1] Well, by the time you had loaded the dram of coal into the truck, your trousers—your trousers were soaking wet when you came out—they were actually frozen to ice by the time you had finished. It was quite an ordeal!

'And the whole set-up of boys—boys were having a pretty lean time of it about then. I think there were more alternatives coming, too. One or two of them had been away to these Government training centres after being in Banwen colliery; and they saw that people could be treated—even if they were young—they could be treated with a little bit more consideration.

'I was involved in the dispute. I didn't know how many got fined. They didn't all get fined. I was one that was fined. I didn't even know I was to pay a fine, because the Labour Officer apparently in those days [war-time] decided. You didn't get any kind of hearing at all. We just had to take the whole thing. When I went home my father was a bit upset, not because of the fine, but because I had made a bit of a spectacle of myself; he and my mother, because they thought I was being involved, hadn't done my work, and had been giving people cheek. They weren't worried because of the fine. Then I went in front of the Agent, Mr Morris. I was going to tell him a lot: I didn't tell him anything! And he said to me that my family, quite a lot of them, who had worked for Evans-Bevan had always worked pretty hard; and, because they were decent people, that it was a shame to me that I had behaved in this way. When I came out, because I hadn't said anything to him, I was in a bit of a stew, now. I didn't realize I was as frightened of him as all that. Because he was quite a formidable character. It wasn't that he'd done anything cruel to anybody, it was just that he had this—he used to wear leggings, leather leggings, you know. And the offices (you see the offices today with carpets and things), he had big polished tables; and a big roaring fire at the back.

'Anyway, I came out; and I went down and volunteered for the army, and the navy—the lot in one day! I got my release from the

[1] The Rhâs is about 800 feet above sea-level.

colliery. They brought in an Act of Parliament that you could leave essential work, but only if you joined the Services. You couldn't just leave to go into a cushy job. So then, William Harris the under-manager (I got on rather well with him), through him I got my release and went into the army.'

When mechanization eventually came it was the obvious physical disadvantages involved in coal-cutter and conveyor that first of all struck the men: Hywel Jeffreys:

'I felt very unsafe when I went on a conveyor. There was something you said, Ifan, about the noise of the conveyors: I didn't realize how much we were depending on our ears when we were working: little cracks in the top, or little flakes dropping by here—things like that, rumbling. So much easier when you were working in a stall. You could say when a place was squeezing, when it was preparing to collapse, settling down or something. You were careful when you heard that. And you could listen for the coal working, and find exactly where was the easiest place to go and pull out a dram of coal. This business of listening: when you are knocking the top. We used to have to hold the mandril firm and tap the top with it; and we could say whether that top was safe or not, just by the sound. The only thing we had to watch for were the *bells*—balls of iron ore that would give a solid sound, and still drop without any warning.

'But I was warned when I went on the conveyor: others had been on conveyors before me, but I was warned! I didn't know how clever they were:

"Oh, you go down by there further."

'They were shoving me further from the gateway so I had a longer way to crawl to my *stent* [stint], my five-yards' stent. Only once they done it! You practically knew what sort of a *face* you had when you had a stall; you knew what was waiting for you every morning. But with a conveyor you didn't know what state it was in; whether you could reach it. It was—when I was working on the conveyor I had to crawl over the back and fore, over the belt and chain and over the *duff* to where I was supposed to start. (The duff was the small coal that was chucked back by the cutter.) The night-shift moved the conveyor forward towards the face, and you didn't know what you'd be seeing in the morning. Sometimes the roof was falling, and sometimes you were shoving over the duff because the oil-lamp wouldn't stand up straight: you had to shove it like that; and the further you had to go the more depressing it was. It wasn't the same as working in the stall: there was no pride in it. With a stall, the more careful you were, the easier the work was. And if you had time to spare, you could timber it up a bit to make things easier for the following day—like sinking the rails down. You know, as you were putting the rails down to run the tram on, you sink the rails down so the tram would be lower to chuck the coal in. Little things like that would help you in filling. If you had to fill with the rails on top of a soft bottom, you were chucking the coal a little bit higher. And if you had a small boy working with you as a mate, it was a big advantage .if you could get the dram over the ends of the rails and grooved in the bottom so he could lift the lumps on easy. Little things like that would make a boy want to work with you, too. Well, he knew you were considering him a bit.

'But when we became mechanized, it was like bringing out the blackguardishness in you. You had to show some sort of aggression or else you'd be kicked from pillar to post. They'd be all on top of you. But with your own stall you could go and look for timber posts if you needed them. But with the conveyor you had to depend on someone else to throw them down to you. You couldn't go back and search for timber: the only thing to do was to sit down until the timber came. And the firemen and officials didn't like that. They were coaxing you to do a bit more, and go and help somebody else to pass the time. But they wanted a place perfectly posted by the end of the shift for the other people to come after you. I never done—I don't think the managers liked me on the conveyor; because I was allowed to go back on to stall-work after two years. I preferred it. But they gave me plenty of rope to kill myself. That's how it was: a tap on the back is worse than a kick sometimes!'

Evan Davies confirmed his friend's estimate of mechanization:

'The craftsmanship went out when mechanization came in. Oh, yes; when that came in it all went. No more clean coal. I've seen them on the surface, on the screens at Onllwyn there. I remember Tom Francis: he used to be on the surface, pulling the slag off the belt. Worked hard and no money. Worked hard and no money.'

Mechanization

By which he meant that there was infinitely more rubbish or slag coming up with the coal, after mechanization; and working on the screens became a very much harder job. But it was George Evans who put his finger on the basic difference under mechanization: it wasn't the surface discomforts caused by the machine but the role of the machine itself:

'But it wasn't, I think, the hardness of the work under the stall-system; maybe the work wasn't so hard. I think the men get rushed around more now under mechanization. The physical things—like dragging those big top-machines about—we were perhaps expected to do a bit too much. But the only drive you had on you was the other man—the boss, which is quite a natural kind of drive to have—another human being. But when you get a machine pushing you, I should imagine they seem to be under a worse strain now than they were then. A man—you can do nothing with a machine, can you?—but you can tell a man, and tell him to go to Hell! You'll feel a little bit better. But you can't do anything to a machine, because they seem to be—well, this is why people like Jeff hark back, although they worked very very hard then. Jeff Camnant was an extremely hard-working man. But he more than probably would rather work the way he used to work in the stalls. Oh yes, and it gave men status, too, you see. They were known for their skill; and it put men—it evened things out. You saw leadership emerging. If a fellow wasn't very good at timbering, he would keep his mouth shut when they were talking about it. You had this natural selection coming along. I notice it now in the construction industry. Dear me! A fellow can shoot his mouth off about anything, because he's never going to have to prove it. I mean, as a collier, I couldn't go saying: "That's the way to timber!" They only had to walk up the road, and they could see my timbering, couldn't they? So if I'm not very good, I keep quiet. So then you got people—and people like Jeff missed this. They made a name for themselves as good timbermen; and, do you know, by the time they became fifty, it makes life quite pleasant for them. Jeff certainly found it. When he was sent down to Cefn Coed it nearly broke his heart. Because he'd been driving the main drift down the *Cornish*[1] for years. He was a man to be accounted with in the *Cornish*. But then he was just one bloke out of many on a rope, pulling it. And in the beginning, he was telling

[1] A seam in Banwen colliery.

169

me himself—and this is what I thought he meant—he made a mistake: he thought that if only he pulled very hard, better than all the rest, he'd be noticed again. But he hadn't got the energy to make his reputation again. His time was past.'

John Williams spent most of his life in stall-work. But he saw the advent of mechanization; and when he became a colliery manager he had, at one period, part of his colliery mechanized and part still on stall-work. He speaks, therefore, with authority about the change-over from mining as a 'handcraft' to full mechanization:

'But the changes that were brought about by the extinction of the stall-work at mechanization were a change of environment more than anything. People were not so contented. Now you work—you and your assistant, a boy, a collier's boy—now if you weren't feeling up to the mark that day, perhaps you'd be hanging back; perhaps you'd be not well enough to carry on the job as usual. But the job was done quietly. Perhaps the man would come in the morning not feeling well; but by half the day he might be feeling right again. But with group-work, as it is with mechaniza-tion, a man feels that he can't go the same pace as somebody else, then he'll say:

"Well, I'd better not go to work today."

'That's a great cause of absenteeism in group-working. In stall-work he'd say:

"I'll go; perhaps I'll come better—half the day, after a few hours." And it was so: he would be better.

'Of course, the biggest point of all was in the beginning—the fear of the workmen that he'd be put out of work by mechaniza-tion. There was a colliery now in the Swansea valley where they were having a coal-cutter in. The management was saying:

"Well, this will cut your coal for you!"

'But the men saw the other picture. They said:

"Well, if this is going to cut the coal, what are we going to work for? If we've only got to fill it, well—they won't need half of us!"

'So this coal-cutter came in on a coal-wagon. The surface-gaffer told a few men: "I want you to unload this." On to a coal-truck, a lower truck, you see. And where the siding was there was the river Twrch passing along; and there was a drop into the river. And what the old fellers did, they went and took this truck down on to the road nearest the river. And they pushed the coal-cutter into the river! The fear was that it was putting men out of work. It wasn't till mechanization was more or less established that men realized they were not as happy as before. There was a different environment altogether. The feeling of a man that he must keep up with the others: in stall-work, if you had a good boy with you, and if you weren't well you'd still carry on with the work, and do your best. And you had the independence of negotiating your own pay with the gaffer. You had to be clever about it, too.' ,

'A lot of the changes are for the good, I expect. But as far as contentment is concerned under trying conditions, I think the miners are much happier in stall-work. There was a better atmosphere all round. I was able to compare it in the colliery I was in, insofar as part of the colliery was on stall-work; and another part on mechanization. I had three drifts: two drifts working on stall-work by the old method, and part on mechanization, conveyor and coal-cutters. And I was able then to observe the difference in attitude of the men on mechanization and the men on stall-work. The man was happier, definitely happier. And then there were these things: you could do something for a man, if he's in a bit of trouble, in stall-work; if he has some domestic difficulty or something like that. You could tell him:

"Leave it for a couple of days; and win your work back."

'An elderly man, not so strong perhaps after years of work—and in those days you were going out of the colliery feet first, not retiring or anything like that, working until you fell! And I did have the satisfaction, many times, of telling old men:

"Now look! Give the stall up, and go out and cut airways. And don't worry."

'And perhaps his work would be less, but he'd be contented. But you couldn't do that with mechanization. Taking all in all, mechanization is capital-intensive: the strain of working in it, especially these days with the latest machinery—you are working with the noise all day; and you are confined in a very small space. And it isn't you that makes the pace of work, it's the machine. I think there's a lot of contentment gone out of the industry. The craft is dictated by the machines. It was a big thing for a man to be told: "Well, you're doing a good job." The under-manager or the manager came along: "I'm quite satisfied with what you're doing here!" On the other hand, perhaps you were ticked off for something; but you wouldn't be ticked off in front of a group.

'There are far greater stresses today than in the old days because the man is not the master of himself. The machine is the master. I think the stresses to a large degree are the cause of absenteeism: a man afraid to meet his master, in a way. Because absenteeism with us on stall-work was very low; and mechanization as it was then was not so tense as it is now. It was far different. Do you know, soldiers are men! Men working in drift-mines, drift-mines closing; and they got to go down the pits. And perhaps they've been in a drift-mine for thirty years: they're a bag of nerves going down the pit, you know, even experienced miners. I've seen them. Abernant colliery, for instance; the drop up there is 2,300 feet. I used to go down there about drainage: I was working the whole area consulting about drainage; I used to meet a lot of old fellows, you know. They couldn't say a word! [Going down in the cage.] The same with mechanization: a lot of them are now working in fear, working in fear every hour of the day. And what can you say then if a man doesn't feel well in the morning, whatever the cause of it: beer, whisky, or over-playing or something like that. He doesn't feel well in the morning: "I'm not going into that mess!"'

'And the humour, of course: the noise washed all that out. Do you know, people who couldn't read or write—but there was something: they could think very deep. And there were lots of them in the early 'twenties. They hadn't—I'll put it like this: they hadn't taken to education very well; but still they had some intelligence; and even men who hadn't taken advantage of education were excellent craftsmen. We think of a man who hasn't been educated as dumb. It's not so!'[1]

Finally, George Evans speaking directly from his own experience, illustrates how the break-up of a work-pattern can alter the framework of a community. Because, as already suggested, the structure of the old stall-system illustrates that 'underground'—the *shape* of the work—had a close relation with the *surface*, the daily life of the village. When, therefore, stall-work was superseded by mechanization certain effects followed inevitably even if, as John Williams observed, they were not at first identified, much less appreciated. This may be a truth that is hardly worth the labouring, but it is too often neglected especially as many sociological studies are prone to concentrate on human relations in an

[1] John Williams's concept of management is, leading the men, instead of pushing them: '*Dewch ac nid Ewch!* [*Come now,* and not, *Go!*]'

abstract way without examining the material culture that underlies and conditions them; and by material culture we posit here not only the present work but the work as it has developed against a historical background.

George Evans:

'Now there is another thing that mechanization has done. It was virtually impossible [under the old stall-system] to be a cheeky boy underground. Now, under mechanization, the boys are put to work in groups; so the boys themselves create their own sort of society; and they can pick on one man and be quite rude to him—an old man. But when the boy—it's true he was in a group to start with, but then he had to go on his own with a man. And they had various ways of putting you in order: they could see your father in the lamp-room; or on a Saturday, if you came in to work and your butty wasn't there, the other men wouldn't take you; and you had to walk home and you wouldn't have any pay. There were no set rules. That was the way it was done. Nobody ever wrote the rules. But they soon put cheeky people in their places; and this was the kind of relationship between man and boy in the colliery.

'That went out with mechanization; and yet there was a great comradeship between man and boy, the man that you worked with. Though some colliers were quite hard. A young boy, say of fourteen, would knock out his oil-lamp and be in the dark: some colliers would say:

"That's all right."

'Other colliers would go screaming because it meant that he had to leave you in the dark and he'd have to walk back to the *lamp-station* to get your light. He couldn't send you back in the dark, and he couldn't go back on his own in the dark, so he had to take the light. Or you had to go back yourself. But normally this wasn't allowed, because the boys weren't allowed to roam around on their own. They had to stay in their place and the man had to go back. Some colliers done it quite humanely, but others used to go through the roof if you were in the dark. Some of those oil-lamps would go out even if you looked at them. I think there were oil-lamps used by boys up until 1942 in Banwen colliery. Boys carried all oil-lamps.'

12

A New Departure?

―――――――――――――※―――――――――――――

Anyone who comes fresh to the activity of taking down on paper or recording on tape what people had told him is bound to ask himself the question: 'Can I accept what I hear as hard historical evidence?' Most of us have been conditioned since childhood to believe more readily what is written or printed: we are inclined to be sceptical about what we hear. There is no better way of putting this scepticism to the test than to record a man describing the work he has been doing for his lifetime, and then to test his account against the relevant books and documents and against one or two informants who have worked at a similar job in the same district and over the same period. Whoever does this is likely to be surprised by the accuracy of the oral material he has collected.

But we have passed the stage when it is necessary to make a detailed justification of oral evidence as opposed to written evidence. The use of oral evidence in history has proved its worth; and we can put forward its usefulness even as a corrective to official records which are generally given full credence, although they are manifestly not all as complete or as accurate as the description *official* would lead us to suppose. The fact they are official does not put them outside a historian's licence to scrutinize and even doubt or question. For there is a great deal of truth in the cynicism that official history is merely a version of what happened as compiled by the winning side: perhaps a barely concealed justification for its continuing to hold power, the title-deeds for an authority to rule. I have always been sceptical of official records ever since taking part in local government—in a very lowly way, in fact at the humblest level of all: the parish- and area parish-councils. While reading the minutes of meetings I had attended I often had the feeling that they were streamlined to the point of appearing to be the record of a different meeting from the one I had attended. Not that there was any blatant inaccuracy that you could pick out (that sort of inaccuracy was usually challenged and corrected before the chairman signed the minutes). In general, what was recorded was an accurate account, as far as it went, of what transpired. But since the time of the meeting so recorded, a selective intelligence had been at work, omitting almost everything that did not contribute to fortifying the main decisions reached: what was said had been carefully sifted to this end. And over the decade or so when I was involved in this work, this streamlining and 'skeletonizing' of minutes increased—understandably, perhaps, owing to the developing size and complexity of local government business. Minutes became barer and more exclusive: the contexts of decisions were omitted, and the record as it now appeared inevitably gave an overall impression that was often more partial to the official view than the actual proceedings justified.

But, apparently, the same tendency is detectable even in the more exalted chambers of government. In a recorded conversation between a former Cabinet Minister, the late Richard Crossman, and the historian, A. J. P. Taylor, the following exchanges occurred:

Mr Crossman: 'I, as you know, am coming out of politics now, partly because I want to write about them again, having been inside. One of the things I've discovered, having read all the Cabinet papers about the meetings I attended, is that the documents often bear virtually no relation to what actually happened. I now know that the Cabinet Minutes are written by Burke Trend,[1] not to say what happened in the Cabinet, but what the Civil Service wishes it to be believed happened, so that a clear directive can be given. Now that's something I presume that historians should know, isn't it?'

Mr Taylor: 'And of which they're well aware. One of the things that a good historian asks is: "Who wrote this? And why did he write it?" There's no such thing as a pure bit of historical evidence.'

Mr Crossman: 'But, Alan, I think I've heard you say that you believe in the written word in the documents. I've discovered that quite often what the press reports about a Cabinet meeting through leaks is probably a great deal more accurate, or tells you

[1] Secretary to the Cabinet.

a great deal more, than the record of the Cabinet as the Cabinet Secretariat put it down.'[1]

If a student of history were to ponder this and find himself wondering: 'If this is true of the official records of the twentieth century, could it not have been true of earlier official records?' his doubts may well be justified. For there must always have been a Secretary to the Cabinet or his equivalent at hand at all levels of government and administration, ready—even eager—to tidy up the report of any event or proceedings, to whittle away the rough edges until it became the credible version of what the presiding power had in mind.

Yet, as implied above, all kinds of evidence have their defects, and the historian who is seeking 'objective', 'scientific' truth is chasing a will o' the wisp. There is not one truth—in the context of history—but many truths, and I believe that the misdirection of much historical work is due to the hubristic assumption that the historian should himself stand outside his *experiment* like the scientist, assuming that the problem he has to examine is out there separate from himself, and that he can effectively insulate himself from it, remaining neutral and objective. But even the physical scientist is involved in his experiment and influences it more than he thinks (he has, for instance, already made a selection, a judgement, by choosing to work in this particular field, doing this particular experiment rather than another). How much more is the historian involved in the period, the events, and the people he is studying? He cannot, therefore, assume that he can attempt to reconstruct the past as if there were already some Platonic *idea* of it laid up in heaven; and that to bring this pattern back to earth he has only to stand off and collect enough facts to make his reconstruction. Yet, however many objective facts he collects, he will still be lacking the mortar to make them hold together.

It would be best for him to admit that he is part of the search himself, that he has to select and interpret, using his own judgement and system of values all the way along. In a sense the historian is better equipped than the scientist because he is dealing chiefly with the doings of men in time, and by a natural empathy he can infer what they were about and what they felt (the scientist has no such direct entry into his material); and it would be more

[1] *Crosstalk*, a BBC television conversation printed in *The Listener*, 1 February 1973, p. 148.

sensible for the historian to come to terms with his own subjectivity. Far from trying to exorcize it, he should recognize it as one of the most valuable instruments in his equipment; and what he finally offers—and can only offer—is an interaction between the data he has collected and his own full being as a man. To his task of trying to reconstruct what it was like to live in a certain time in the past he then brings all his faculties, subjective and objective: his scholarship, his judgement, his scepticism, his sympathy and intuition, and finally a mite of imagination which is probably the most vital element in the whole array. It is true that this view of history has great dangers for those who follow it; but the dangers are plain to see, and it is certainly an approach that is not more hazardous than for those who cling to the reductive-objective view of history which has been known to betray its adherents into activities like trying to recapture the past in a tight net of numbers. On the contrary, I believe the dangers are greater for these historians: for having *Quantification* and *Enumeration* painted on each side of the prow they have been lulled into believing that their craft will take them anywhere, and that they can fish far and wide with the confidence that it can never be upturned by any adverse winds of criticism, weight and number always conspiring to keep it on an even keel.

This is not to say, however, that the technique of using oral sources has to be given respectable credentials as if it is being introduced into history for the first time. It has, indeed, a long lineage, and we need only remind ourselves that much early history (including a great deal of the Bible!) is simply oral tradition committed to parchment or paper. But there are also more recent examples in historiography. The first that comes to mind is Richard Gough's *History of Myddle* in Shropshire. Professor W. G. Hoskins wrote a stimulating introduction to this book when it was recently reissued:

'It is, in fact, a unique book. It gives us a picture of seventeenth-century England in all its wonderful and varied detail such as no other book that I know even remotely approaches. If History is, as has once been said, the men and women of the past talking and we overhearing their conversations, then Gough's history of his native parish, written between the years 1700 and 1706, is History.'[1]

[1] The Centaur Press, Ltd., Fontwell, Sussex, 1968, p. 1.

The first section of the book is conventional local history; but then Gough breaks fresh ground by taking the pews in the village church as a plan for the second part of his book. The pews at that time (as they were in many rural parishes in England until recent years) were allocated to the owners or tenants of each farm or holding in the parish. Gough had the original idea of writing all he knew about the occupants of each pew. A great deal of what he wrote is, as Professor Hoskins pointed out, nothing more than gossip, usually of a scandalous nature; and Gough during his long life in Myddle must have gone about the village making a mental note of innumerable tales, and writing them up later. They make absorbing reading, and give a telling picture of the times, having all the colour and the detail, the immediacy of an account told you directly by a practised narrator. For gossip though highly subjective is, as Professor Hoskins notes, 'one of the most important sources for the historian who has any imaginative insight into the past'.

Gough was a contemporary of John Aubrey whose taste for historical gossip was exactly similar. But Aubrey was writing about people at a higher social level, people who were near the centre of things, who were 'in the news'; and for that reason he is better known than Gough. But they both used the same method: hearing, and later writing down stories and titbits of information about various people they came into contact with: this is what Aubrey undoubtedly did in his *Brief Lives*, and he appears to have done this for most of his own life. As Oliver Lawson Dick wrote in his edition of Aubrey's *Brief Lives*: 'His taste for historical gossip appeared early, too. For he mentions that "when a Boy he did ever love to converse with old men as Living Histories"; and it was particularly to his mother's parents, Isaac and Israel Lyte, that he turned for information'.[1] And Aubrey often repeats the following phrase in his writings: 'When I was a little boy before the Civil Warres'. I have heard a similar phrase many times from the older generation in East Anglia: 'That were afore the First War' or 'That were afore I went into the Army'. The First World War was as sharp a watershed in our time as the seventeenth-century Civil Wars were to Aubrey and his contemporaries.

The third, and great, figure who used the technique of going to

[1] In the Introduction, 'The Life and Times of John Aubrey', London, 1949, p. xxix.

living people for historical evidence and inspiration is Sir Walter Scott. If anyone has any doubts about this, the verses from Robert Burns with which Scott prefaced many of his novels should dispel them:

> *Hear Land o' Cakes and brither Scots,*
> *Frae Maidenkirk to Johnny Groat's,*
> *If there's a hole in a' your coats,*
>   *I rede ye tent it;*
> *A chiel's amang you takin' notes*
>   *An' faith he'll prent it.*[1]

But Scott did not start his first novel until 1805 when he was thirty-four. For years before, he had been travelling the Border Country in the course of his work as a lawyer, listening to the tales of the events still recent in men's memories. Having first been sensitized by reading Bishop Percy's *Reliques of Ancient English Poetry*, he continued purposefully to roam the countryside with his friend Robert Shortreed, looking for popular ballads. He published these in 1802 under the title *Minstrelsy of the Scottish Border*. He knew the Border Country well, for when he was a very young child his father had sent him there from Edinburgh. He had contracted poliomyelitis, and he went to his grandfather's farm at Sandyknowe in Tweed-dale to recover. The Border scene with its towers, legends and colourful oral tradition etched itself into the consciousness of the young Scott; he got an early glimpse of the Scotland he was to immortalize. At the same time as he was later collecting the Border ballads, he was also visiting the Highlands and talking to Jacobites who had taken part in the '45 Rebellion. Scott recognized through conversing with these old men—perhaps better than anyone then living—what had really happened as a result of the '45. Culloden saw the end of a culture: the dispersal or the destruction of the Highland clans, a tribal society and a way of life that had lasted in unbroken continuity since the Iron Age. The old men he talked to were truly historical documents; and contact with them undoubtedly helped to give his writing that veracity that informs his earlier novels like *Waverley, The Antiquary, Rob Roy* and *Guy Mannering*. In his fifth novel, *Old Mortality*, Scott went farther back than the memories

---

[1] *I rede ye tent it* = I advise you to tend to it.
  Chiel' = a young fellow (chield or child); *prent* = print.

of the men he had talked to—back into the seventeenth century, to the conflict between the Covenanters, and the Royalists and Episcopalians. And if Scott's historical credibility needs to be tested, one has only to read or re-read *Old Mortality* and set the book alongside what has been happening in Northern Ireland during the past few years. How aptly does the seventeenth-century phrase, *The Killing Time*, fit these present years when the bigotry and violence of the seventeenth century have re-erupted in that province.

Professor Hugh Trevor-Roper was the first to reaffirm Sir Walter Scott's importance to history. He points out in two lectures that Scott initiated an entirely new approach to history, and influenced historians and writers throughout Europe. He said:

'It may seem odd that a novelist should be credited with a historical revolution. But historical revolutions are not made by historians. Historians are technicians who may refine their tools and dig further and deeper along the channels within which they work; but generally speaking, it is not they who point the new directions in which those channels shall be dug. Those who have redirected the course of history have almost all been non-historians or, at most amateur historians: Machiavelli, Montesquieu, Herder, Hegel, Marx. And Sir Walter Scott, I shall suggest, was a historical innovator in this sense.'[1]

In his other lecture Professor Trevor-Roper shows that Scott was doing in his novels essentially the same thing as the German, Niebuhr, in his historical writings: 'Both used a new insight to reconstruct, out of hitherto neglected material, the vanished context of formal history. Implicit in the work of both was a new historical philosophy. Unlike the classical "philosophic historians", they saw the successive ages of the past not as mere stages in the history of progress, whose values lay in their relevance to the present, but as self-sufficient totalities of human life, valid within their own terms, demanding from the historian neither praise nor blame but sympathetic, imaginative re-creation. Such re-creation required effort. The historian must breathe the atmosphere of the past, think in its mental categories.'[2]

[1] *Sir Walter Scott and History*, a BBC broadcast lecture, printed in *The Listener*, 19 August 1971, p. 226.
[2] *The Romantic Movement and the Study of History*, The Athlone Press, 1968, p. 13.

Both, that is, by their methods implied that historical truth is not the monopoly of the library or the muniment room; and Scott by his own practice, demonstrated that historical enlightenment, at least, is more likely to be obtained from becoming acquainted with the actual physical environment of historical events, with that part of the material culture that has survived, and—most important of all—from talking to the survivors of the way of life that was just going under. Scott had close contact with all ranks of the society in which he grew up—a society compounded of the old and the new—from poachers to the aristocracy: he knew not only in his head how the old society worked, he knew it in his bones. Frequent talks with survivors of the old Scotland that was quickly disappearing gave him a historical sensitivity that he could have acquired from no other source.

There are many other writers since Scott who used this method of taking historical information, potential or actual, from living people. Henry Mayhew, in the mid-nineteenth century, Charles Booth and Seebohm Rowntree later; and George Sturt (Bourne) was recording at the beginning of this century an old community that was vanishing from near-metropolitan Farnham fifty years before the same type of community was being displaced in other, more rural parts of Britain. All these writers had one thing in common: they were using this method of taking evidence from people during periods that had a similar character. They were all writing during the stress periods of history—Gough and Aubrey during the turmoil of the Civil Wars, Scott at the end of the old Scotland and the emergence of the new, the nineteenth-century writers when the Industrial Revolution was causing turbulence and want in town and city; lastly, the writers today, who are living —here and in America—in societies that are under like strain caused by the lightning changes following two World Wars, and the leap forward of technology.

But this process of rapid change, after its first assault, appears instinctively to evoke a saving counter-movement; just as an organic body quickly mobilizes its forces against too rapid a disturbance either in its internal or external environment. The oral history movement is only part of the widespread interest in the past that extends throughout all classes of society at the present time, embracing old engines, old implements, old pictures, photographs, clothes, songs, buildings—almost any aspect of the prior culture that is in danger of being forgotten or lost altogether.[1] Yet the past has always been with us. Why then are we so conscious of it at a time like the present? Perhaps it is because in smoother times we are not so much aware of the past; but now that it is slipping away—like the passing of a friend we have grown up with—its particular qualities come to the fore, come into perspective against the background of a newly emerging scene. We then value these qualities the more, and we seek to record them, to preserve, if not to conserve.

Most of the examples of oral history given here are designed to show the scope that this technique possesses, how over a wide field it can give the *inside view* that is so valuable in social history. But we must beware of making exaggerated claims for this new development or of over-emphasizing its importance in the wealth of fresh sources it can unearth. What oral history does admirably in this respect is to supplement, supplying extra sources for conventional history by salvaging the sort of material that tends to slip between the meshes of print or documentation. Only very occasionally, in my experience, does it uncover new areas altogether. As can be recognized from many of the examples given here, they are the marginalia, even the trivia, of social history, but whose collection and inclusion among the sources can nevertheless be justified by their helping, even as small insignificant details, to give the historian that insight into a past that only recently passed out of his immediate reach; in helping to convince him, moreover, that this past, in spite of its proximity, had an entirely different ambience from the time we are living in now, informed as it was with different values and supported by entirely different assumptions.

It is here, I believe, that the greatest value of oral history lies: in the sense of enlightenment that a student can obtain by working in a community whose survivors still have in their memories the lineaments of a society that has been supplanted, but where the remnants of the material culture of that society—the tools, the machines, buildings, the photographs and so on—are still there to reinforce those memories. It is this side-effect, while the student is acquiring his new sources, that is of first importance in oral history, because it is from this direct contact that he will get the sense of history that he cannot acquire by an effort of will but

[1] *Where Beards Wag All*, p. 279.

which comes only through a kind of osmosis, enabling him to win his own personal understanding of the past which is the first requisite, it seems to me, of a historian—that electric charge that can induce a ground-pattern in the facts he has collected, and can make his contribution a real re-creation and not simply a pedestrian academic exercise of describing the past by accumulating masses of disparate facts. But even if he is not granted this, at least he is doing his own research, making his own sources, and this in itself will give him a greater sense of involvement and discovery. Yet too many are content merely with a collection of data: admittedly these are of first importance, but once they are collected, the real problem remains: the need to find a new angle, a new way of looking at the facts. This, it seems to me, is the creative essence of history; for to understand the past to make it come alive, each age has continually to re-interpret it. Through contact with living people it seems more likely that the student will get that little bit extra, that trace-element of imagination, the supererogatory grace, sense of history—call it what you will—that will make his work more pleasurable to himself and its presentation more acceptable to those who read it.

If, therefore, the student should aim to get something more than oral sources while he is collecting information, it follows that his approach to his informant is vital. For instance, by calling a meeting with a man or woman an *interview* he has already formalized it, whereas to get the best results the meeting should be as informal as possible; it should be a talking together, a conversing, not between *the* man up here and *a* man down there, as the very word interview seems to imply, but a talk between two people on the same level, two equals sharing, at least for the time of their conversation, a common absorbing interest. It is only in this context that we get the real flow of information that does something more than skim the surface for the facts that happen to be floating around. And it is only in the kind of relation where the seeker does not attempt to dominate the talk, but merely to guide it by an occasional well-directed question or comment, that we get that spate of reminiscence that can carry insight along with it. To follow the daily example of radio and television would be disastrous for the student of oral history; for in these media we hear or see the microphone often being used as an aggressive implement, like a kind of hand-grenade. But in fairness it should be said that the interviewers in the broadcasting media are constrained by the lack of time, but also—I sometimes think—by a faulty style or tradition. So, too, should one sociological method of collecting evidence be avoided as a model. Here the purpose is avowedly extractive: information is usually sought under different heads; the aim is often to get as wide as possible a sample, and the time spent with each informant minimal. The interviewer is not much interested in the person as a person; but is—so to speak —flipping over the index until he gets the information he wants: he has no time to read the book.

The best method of getting historical information from people, in my view, is that practised by the professional collectors in the Department of Irish Folklore in Dublin, The Welsh Folk Museum at St Fagans, Cardiff, The School of Scottish Studies in Edinburgh and The Institute of Dialect and Folk Life Studies at the University of Leeds. In 1970, and again in 1974, I spent some time with James Delaney, a collector in the Irish Folklore Department, going round with him visiting his people in the district, the midlands of Eire. His informants were all expertly chosen in the first place, and he visited them regularly: they were all his friends, and would have been greatly put out if he had passed their door without looking in. He had been visiting the older ones regularly for many years, recording them through notebook and tape, and an occasional film; writing up each visit for the archives. This is real recording in depth—admittedly in what is still a rich historical environment, one of the richest in western Europe. This is undoubtedly the ideal method of trying to re-create any culture that has substantially disappeared. It is the method used by the anthropologists: of living as far as possible with the people you are studying. Indeed, it has an advantage over classical anthropology in that the collector is studying the culture from the *inside*, as part of it, not as a rather clinical observer.

But there is a great danger here of trying to lay down the law, attempting to formalize the maieutics of oral history and to reduce them to rules. It is far better for each student to make his own rules, or at least as few rules as he makes in meeting a person— that is, no rules at all except the instinctive 'rule' of courtesy and a particular accommodation to the speaker. He will do best if he finds his own way, adopting through trial and error the manner that suits him best. It is salutary to remind ourselves that the classifiers are always lying in wait to tidy up anything that has the appearance of being new.[1] We are already hearing a great deal about methodology which in essence is no more than 'the stone in stone-soup'. The secret of mastering the technique of collecting oral evidence is no secret at all: it is simple, as C. G. Jung pointed out in another connection: 'In reality everything depends on the man, and little or nothing on the method'; and he quotes a Chinese aphorism as a warning: 'If the wrong man uses the right means, the right means work in the wrong way.'[2] And it would be possible to extend this by adding in relation to oral history: 'Concentrate on *your* man—the informant—and the method will look after itself.'

The same principle applies to the transcription of recordings as to the recording itself. To get its full virtue the historian in the first place has to record, do the actual work himself. Less than in any form of historical research can the exploration of oral sources be done vicariously. To get the extra bonus mentioned above, the student, perforce, has to be involved himself. The same argument applies to the making of the transcript. Laborious as this work is, it is best that he do it himself; for this reason: by its very slowness this task has the advantage of making him re-live the conversation, often bringing to his notice the nuances that he had missed at the time, and which would escape him perhaps entirely were the tape he recorded to be transcribed by someone else and given to him in typescript. Transcribing of the countryman by the person who did the recording is essential in my view because of the language. Only he can do it satisfactorily; and even then it often means that he will have to return to the speaker two or three times in an attempt to get the meaning of some words or phrases. But each visit of this kind is likely to bring its own reward.

---

[1] 'Take up the catalogue of courses issued by any of our great multiversities—the mills of our "knowledge industry"—and there you find the whole repertory of expertise laid out. And does it not cover every inch of the cultural ground with scientized specialization? What is there left that the non-expert can yet be said to know? Name it—and surely it will soon be christened as a new professional field of study with its own jargon and methodology, its own journals and academic departments.' Theodore Roszak, *Where the Wasteland Ends*, Faber and Faber, 1973, pp. 34–35.

Although this was written about the United States, it is a warning light that can be seen and appreciated over here.

[2] *Alchemical Studies*, London, 1967, p. 7.

A New Departure?

To revert to the place of oral sources within the framework of conventional history: it has already been suggested that collecting this kind of information tends to induce a synoptic view of the whole context of the topic you are pursuing. Your search widens out and shows the inter-relatedness of the material you are studying with other peripheral aspects that, at first glance, might appear irrelevant. It demonstrates people and processes in movement and not frozen still as has become the accepted practice in conventional history. A lot has been gained, I submit, by taking first-hand accounts of the hay-trade from survivors, as described in a previous book.[1] Through them the trade is placed in its social setting; and their narratives help to bring back the period vividly, giving the feeling of what the road was like both during the day and the night: the early morning town comes alive, and the pubs are brought in as essential elements in the scene; and the unexpected links with fishing and other occupations illustrate how widely these connections extend.

But suppose we were to study the hay-trade solely in the orthodox way of history departments in many universities. The first thing to do is to isolate the trade and hay itself from its context. Then get the figures. How many hay-dealers were engaged in the trade? From where did they operate? We'll have a distribution map here, perhaps two: one to show where the hay grew, and one to show where it was collected and marketed; then the quantity. How much hay was sold? We'll have some tables, some graphs, some diagrams—and so on and so on. Yet what comes out of it all is that an immense amount of work has been expended, and the result does nothing very much more than to dot the i-s and cross the t-s of what we know already. It is not suggested here that this sort of approach is not valid: but it should not be implied, by the importance given to it, that it is the only proper and up-to-date approach to history. Wherever it is applied it should be pointed out that it is only one kind of approach, and a very partial approach at that. By overplaying this reductive type of research many university departments have contributed to the ossification of historical studies; and where it is used, it should be balanced by a more 'social', less selective approach which tends to make the student aware of the inter-relatedness of historical phenomena as opposed to their isolation or neat pigeon-holing. But I suspect

[1] *The Days That We Have Seen,* Chapter 4.

that this reductivism has been so fashionable because of the un-conscious wish to gain some of the kudos and respectability the natural sciences have won for themselves during this century; and it gains powerful support from the widespread assumption that modern science has the answer for everything that man really needs to know. But it is a false premise to expect a humanity like history to have the same sort of base as a natural science where counting, weighing and measuring are the very kernel of the technique; and their application to the study of history is bound to have a severely limited scope.

A breaking away, however, from this objective, 'scientific' view of history has become apparent during the last few years; and many prominent historians have become critical of the conventional view of history. The increasing interest in oral history and the rediscovery of Sir Walter Scott are signs that orthodoxy is once more being called into question. Not only Professor Hugh Trevor-Roper but another Oxford historian has drawn attention to Scott's importance for present-day students of history. He writes:

'True history begins with Sir Walter Scott. He felt himself backwards into time. He did not always succeed. *Ivanhoe* is not a convincing picture of the Middle Ages: it is simply lay figures in fancy dress. But *Old Mortality* is a convincing picture of the later seventeenth century. It is the cloak from which we are all cut. That the past is different from the present is a hard doctrine.'[1]

The unease with which many people regard the teaching of history both in schools and universities is due in great part to the way history has moved away from men and women and has be-dimmed itself in clouds of abstraction and over-intellectualizing. Anthony Richard Wagner, Garter King of Arms, in a stimulating first chapter to a new edition of his book on genealogy, has made this point clearly:

'History is too commonly regarded as abstract and detached rather than continuous with ourselves, a dimension without which we cannot see our own lives in the round. . . . The heirs of the Industrial Revolution can feel themselves cut off from an older England almost like men of another race. Yet, when these same people perceive their derivation step by step, through their own lineage, from men of so different a world, yet of their own blood,

[1] A. J. P. Taylor, *The Times Literary Supplement*, 23 March 1973, p. 327.

they may see both themselves and the past in a new conjunction and perspective. This explains, at least in part, the trouble and effort with which the dispossessed of the countryside, later enriched by industry, will pursue their links with their lost past. For the imagination of surprisingly many modern Englishmen pre-industrial England has the quality of a lost home.'[1]

Whether it is through the descent of the family, through the work of the family, or through an aspect of the familiar environment, oral history can help to resolve the crisis that is endemic in the teaching of history. Contact with a living community that contains survivors of an already historical era will help to emphasize that history is a corporate discipline that has been too much fragmented. For the dangers of specialization are obvious to anyone who is interested in oral sources. If you are a specialist and nothing else you tend to plough your own furrow and to get deeper and deeper and to lose sight of the countryside and the people around. And once you have lost sight of people, as a historian you are truly lost, for history is first and last a humanity, not a discipline vainly straining to win the prestige of a natural science.

[1] *English Genealogy,* Oxford University Press, 1972, p. 3. Note in this connection, the popularity of 'country' books within the last few decades.

Appendix

---------*---------

Mr W. R. Ward (Chapter Four) has lost most of his sight during recent years. Therefore he composes his poems without writing a word on paper. Few of the later ones I recorded have ever been written down. At least one of the following poems is transcribed for the first time.

The Old Station Bus

The other night I had a dream,
No silly nonsense or fuss,
I dreamt it was nineteen hundred and two:
I was driving the old horse-bus.

The bus—it was called the Station Bus—
Did meet all trains, and more:
It took passengers from the Station
To their lodgings or front door.

The boards around its top did say:
To Any Part of Town;
And folk saw visitors come and go
When the bus went up or down.

The passengers they rode inside;
The baggage was on top.
When several families arrived,
Of trunks there were a lot.

There were tin-trunks and cabin-trunks,
Round-topped ones, large and small;
There were gladstone bags and carpet-bags
And a thing they called *hold-all*.

They were all hoisted to the top,
And often stacked so high
That strangers they would stop and stare
When the bus did pass them by.

A local wit was heard to say:
'If young Bill will stack so high,
To make room for the bus to go
They'll have to raise the sky!'

The Farm Wagon

How sad to see you neglected,
Fast falling in to decay,
The bushes grown tall about you:
You're almost hidden away.

The craftsmen that shaped your felloes
And turned your beautiful naves,
If they could see you neglected,
Surely they'd turn in their graves.

The day that you left the workshop,
Resplendent in red and brown:
The pride of a cheerful carter
On his journeys to the town.

In your shafts two lovely horses,
Old Bragg and the younger Gyp.
One hand held the reins to guide them,
The other a brass-bound whip.

A plate still fixed to a panel
Shows a former owner's name:
John Goddard, Farmer of Tunstall,
Of agricultural fame.

How sad to see you neglected,
Cast aside, as one might say.
Though horses and carter have passed on,
There's beauty in your decay.

Wild Fowling

The ebbing river narrows;
The mud-flats are left bare.
The wild-fowl are searching them
For the food that could be there.

The curlews rise upon the wing,
And when darkness fills the sky
And as they fly towards the flats,
We hear the curlews' cry.

They light upon the mud-flats;
Join the wild duck and the teal,
Already there before them,
Seeking their evening meal.

The curlews push their long bills
Into the sand and mud,
Searching for the worms that live there,
The sand-worms and the lugs.

The birds search round in the darkness
Without a thought of fear.
But when the moon rises in the sky,
Danger is quite often near.

For the fowler waits behind the bank,
Watching the birds draw near;
And when they come within gun's range,
It's the fowler's gun they hear.

The birds that did not feel the sting
Of the fowler's lethal shot,
Now quickly rise upon the wing,
Fly off to a safer spot.

The fowler's dog now search for dead and wounded:
He searches the flats far and wide;
And cease not in his duty
Till the birds are brought to his master's side.

The fowler puts the birds in his bag:
Their number he has counted.
He reaches down to pick up his gun,
Walks back to his home contented.

Selected Written Sources

———————————— ✳ ————————————

Aubrey, John, *Brief Lives*, edited with an Introduction by Oliver Lawson Dick, Secker and Warburg, 1949

Chaplin, Sid, *Durham Mining Villages*, Working Papers in Sociology, No. 3, Department of Sociology, University of Durham

Douglass, Dave, *Pit Talk in County Durham* and *Pit Life in County Durham*, (two) History Workshop Pamphlets, Ruskin College, Oxford

Edwards, Ness, *History of the South Wales Miners' Federation*, Lawrence and Wishart, 1938

Gough, Richard, *The History of Myddle* (Introduction by Professor W. G. Hoskins), Centaur Press, 1968

Hopkin, Deian (editor), *Llafur*, Journal of the Society for the Study of Welsh Labour History, Department of History, University College, Swansea

Hurley, Jack, *Rattle His Bones* (A Century of Poor Law), The Exmoor Press, Dulverton, Somerset

Lukacs, Georg, *The Historical Novel*, Peregrine Books, 1969

Mayhew, Henry, *Mayhew's Characters*,
                 Mayhew's London,
                 London's Underworld, Spring Books (each book edited by Peter Quennell)

Mitchell, Hannah, *The Hard Way Up*, Faber and Faber, 1968

Morgan, John E., *A Village Workers' Council* (Windsor Lodge, S.W.M.F., Ynysybwl), Celtic Press, Pontypridd

Moss, W. M., *Oral History Program Manual*, Praeger, N.Y., Pall Mall Press, London, 1974

North, F. J., *Coal and the Coalfields of Wales*, Welsh National Museum, 1931

Oral History: An Occasional News Sheet (1–5), editor, Dr Paul Thompson

Oral History (twice yearly), editor, Dr Paul Thompson, The University of Essex, Wivenhoe Park, Colchester, C04 2SQ

Oral History News Letter, Oral History Association, University of California, Los Angeles

Oral History Review (annual) University of Vermont, Burlington, Vermont, 05401, U.S.A.

Roszak, Theodore, *Where the Wasteland Ends*, Faber and Faber, 1972

Sanderson, Stewart F., (editor) *Theses and Dissertations in Folk Life Studies*, The University of Leeds, 1961–70

Shumway, Gary, *Oral History in the United States : A Directory*, The Oral History Association, New York, 1971

South Wales Coalfield History Project Final Report. Departments of History and Economic History, University College, Swansea, 1974

Thompson, Paul, *The Edwardians*, Weidenfeld and Nicolson, 1975

Vansina, J., *Oral Tradition : A Study in Historical Methodology*, London, 1961

Waserman, M. J., *Bibliography in Oral History*, Oral History Association, New York, 1971

Widdowson, J. D. A. (editor), *Lore and Language*, Department of English Language, The University, Sheffield, S10 2TN

Index

---------------- ✳ ----------------

Index

Index

market days, 33–4, 44, 45
Marx, Karl, 180
Masson, Meg G., 105–18
Maugham, Somerset, 83
Mayhew, Henry, 181
mechanization, coal-mining, 122–3, 164–73
Members of Parliament, 26, 30
Middle English, 19
Miller, Douglas, 126
mills, weaving, 24–30
mining, 121–73 *passim*; absenteeism, 170, 172; anecdotes about, 143–51; anthracite collieries, 128–73 *passim*; boys working in, 124–5, 126, 129–42, 145–6, 164–6, 168, 173; coalcutters and conveyors, 122, 125, 127, 167–73; door-boys, 145–6; drams, 122, 126; drilling tools, 140–2; falls and accidents, 123, 127–8, 133, 150–1, 167; foreign workers, 146–7; go-slow protests, 143–4; hierarchy underground, 159–60; influence of chapel, 155–6; lamps, 126–7, 131, 134, 160, 173; mechanization, 122–3, 164–73; nationalization, 158; owners, 153–8; pneumoconiosis, 122, 127, 145; price list, 152–8, 161–3; screening, 130, 168–9; silicosis, 145; skills of, 136–42; stall system, 122–3, 125–6, 135–6, 159–60, 167–72; steam-coal collieries, 129; tools, 140–2; use of timber, 137–39; victimization, 160–3
Montesquieu, 180
motor-cars, introduction of, 31, 33, 34
Mountain Ash, 124–8
mourning dress, 64, 91
Myddle, 177–8

National Coal Board, 160
National Physical Laboratory, Teddington, 105
nationalization, coal industry, 158

Netherway, Gwen, 127–8
Newnham Park, 70–1
Nicholas, Shôb, 165
Niebuhr, 180
night-soil, 32
North, A., 98
Norwich, 34–5, 87

official records, as an historical source, 174–6
Ogilvies' estate, 56
Oldham, 30
Onllwyn colliery, 128, 141, 148, 168
operatics, 30
oral history, early examples of, 177–81; methods and techniques, 65–6, 88–9, 129, 182–5; and official records, 174–6; towns as source of, 20–1; transcribing, 185; value of, 17–20, 21, 152, 182–4, 186–9
Orford, 48
Otley, 117
Oulton Broad, 61, 63
Outney Common, 38
oxen, 56

Palmer, Eric, 83
Papendiek, Mrs, 99
Parliamentary elections, 26, 30
Pausanias, 102
Percy, Bishop, 179
Peterloo, 27
pneumoconiosis, 122, 127, 145
Powley, Happy, *see* Sturgeon, Happy
Powley, Jack, 71
Powley, Mary, 78
prams, men pushing, 36
Pratt, Robert G., 41
printing works, 36
public-houses, effect of motor-car on, 34
Pugh, Tom, 145–6

Redgrave family, 38
Redhouse Farm, Aldeburgh, 56

17

666K

W